EDWARD DUFFIELD NEILL: PIONEER EDUCATOR

EDWARD DUFFIELD NEILL

A Daguerreotype taken in 1849
Courtesy of the Minnesota Historical Society

EDWARD DUFFIELD NEILL: PIONEER EDUCATOR

by

HUNTLEY DUPRE

MACALESTER COLLEGE PRESS
Saint Paul, Minnesota

PRINTED BY THE LUND PRESS, INC., MINNEAPOLIS, MINNESOTA

To

CHARLES J. TURCK
Citizen and Educator of
Vision and Courage

Preface

THIS historical essay presumes to be a modest chapter in the history of education in the United States in general and in Minnesota in particular, as illustrated personally in the education of Edward Duffield Neill in the East, and in his career as a pioneer in education on the frontier, adapting traditional education to the needs of men under new conditions, and according to his concepts of education, morality and religion in a democracy. In no sense is this monograph intended to be a biography of Neill or a treatment of his career as a missionary, organizer of churches, historian, or public servant.

When the author started his research on Neill in the autumn of 1946, he did not connect the end result with the Centennial, but he is very happy that this study appears one hundred years after the establishment of the Territory of Minnesota and in the very month of 1849 in which Neill arrived in St. Paul to take up his life's work.

For such a slight volume I (becoming personal) am under unusual obligation to a number of persons. To my friend, Philip D. Jordan, I am deeply indebted for his great interest and valuable suggestions both for content and for a workmanlike and artistic publication. I am very grateful for the steady interest and material assistance of Elmer E. Engelbert. I profited by the wise counsel of Bertha L. Heilbron, editor of *Minnesota History*. I am under great obligation to the staff of the Minnesota Historical Society, particularly to Russell F. Barnes, Lucile Kane, and G. Hubert Smith, for their many courtesies in connection with my use of the rich resources of the Society. My thanks are due to Beaumont Newhall of Rochester, N. Y., for illustrations; to my colleague, Alfred P. Maurice, for his art work; to Andrew W. Anderson, Joseph W. Cochran, William P. Kirkwood, and Edward J. Moles for sharing with me their vivid recollections of Neill; to Mrs. Jean Wetterlin Watson for her genuine interest and competent typing; and to my wife for her unflagging encouragement and valuable assistance throughout.

HUNTLEY DUPRE

TABLE OF CONTENTS

LIST OF ILLUSTRATIONS

The Making of the Man

The Making of the Man

EDWARD DUFFIELD NEILL was undoubtedly the most persistent and single-minded champion of education, both private and public, Christian and secular, in early Minnesota, from his arrival in 1849, the year of the establishment of the Territory, at the age of twenty-six, to his death in 1893. Although he was an ordained minister of the Presbyterian Church and came to the Territory of Minnesota as a home missionary, his true life-work was education.

Neill may "well be named Minnesota's apostle of education," wrote William Watts Folwell, the first president (1869–1884) and true founder of the University, and historian of the state.[1] A mere enumeration of Neill's offices supports this judgment. He was one of the first trustees of education and the first secretary of the Board of Education of St. Paul, the first Superintendent of Schools of the Territory, the founder of Baldwin School and of the College of St. Paul, the Superintendent of Public Instruction in the new state, the first chancellor of the yet-unorganized University of Minnesota, the founder and provost of the short-lived Jesus College, the founder of Macalester College, and its professor of history, English literature, and political economy. Late in life he gave extension lectures, in conformity with his vision of adult education. In productive scholarship, he was a prolific author of historical treatises.

Neill adapted to the new northwest the rich heritage of privately-endowed education in the East, of which he was a product. Two years at the University of Pennsylvania, a bachelor's degree from Amherst, a period of teaching in Virginia, a year at Andover Seminary, and private instruction in Philadelphia for the ministry gave him the broad and deep foundations for his career in religion, in education, and in public service in Minnesota and in the nation.

The Neills were descended on both the maternal and paternal sides from early Scotch-Irish Presbyterian settlers in Delaware. Edward Neill's great-grandfather, John Neill, a lawyer from the north of Ireland, was in Delaware as early as 1739. His second son, John (1749–1816), a physician, established himself at Snow Hill, Worcester County, Maryland. The latter's only son, Henry (1783–1845), the father of Edward D. Neill, was also a physician, having gotten his medical degree from the University of Pennsylvania. In 1806 he married Martha, the daughter of Dr. Benjamin Duffield, a distinguished physician of Philadelphia.

This worthy couple had ten children, nine of whom lived relatively long lives, and of whom Edward was the fifth son and the next to last child. Two of the six sons were physicians, two were ministers, one was an army captain, and the youngest was Brevet Brigadier General in the United States Army, and at one time was commandant of cadets at West Point, from which he had graduated and where he had taught. The oldest brother, Benjamin Duffield, had earned his B.A., at Yale in 1830, and his M.D., at the University of Pennsylvania. The second brother, Henry, studied at the University of Pennsylvania, earned his B.A., at Amherst in 1834, and did his theological work at Lane Theological and Andover Seminaries. He had churches in Hatfield and Lenox, Massachusetts, in Detroit, in Geneseo, New York, and in New Brunswick, New Jersey. He married Lucy Humphrey, daughter of Heman Humphrey, president of Amherst College, when Edward was a student in that institution. The third son, John, earned the B.A., M.A., and Ph.D., degrees at the University of Pennsylvania, where he subsequently taught clinical surgery.

The character of Edward's father is revealed in the eulogy by the editor of the Philadelphia *North American*, written on the occasion of the father's death on October 7, 1845:

> The obsequies of the lamented Dr. Henry Neill were yesterday attended by a large concourse of citizens, at the promptings of unfeigned respect for the character of the deceased. It was a tribute to blameless integrity of life, benevolence of feeling, principle and action; modesty of deportment, which while it acknowledged all excellence in others sought no distinction for himself, all springing from that love of God, and love to man which adorned his life and shed heavenly peace over his soul as he resigned his spirit to his Saviour.[2]

The good doctor's pastor, Rev. Albert Barnes, of the First Presbyterian Church in Philadelphia, who had a great influence upon Edward Neill, characterized the father in his memorial address on October 19:

. . . He was eminently what the physician aims to be. . . . He was formed for friendship. His heart was warm and open, and steady and without suspicion. . . . In his profession, as in his whole walk he was modest, unobtrusive, and retiring, he used no arts to gain popularity. . . . Rare is it that men die in whose character there is so little to regret, or whose life may be recalled with so much unalloyed pleasure. . . ."[3]

It was into this devout family with its long service to the liberal professions of the law, medicine, and now the ministry, that Edward Duffield Neill was born on August 9, 1823. Edward Neill was nurtured in a home whose members had the deep respect for learning shared by the great numbers of Scotch-Irish in the middle colonies as a central part of their heritage from Calvin and Knox. In fact, Charles F. Thwing writes: "The first force in point of time as well as in respect to efficiency, making for the higher education [in the middle colonies], was religion, and religion took the form of Presbyterianism."[4]

The historical colleges were already well established by the time young Neill was ready to matriculate in the University of Pennsylvania. The need for educated ministers led to the chartering of Princeton (College of New Jersey) in 1745, controlled by Presbyterians but not officially affiliated with the Presbyterian Synod. This fourth college (after Harvard, William and Mary, and Yale) to be founded in the colonies was followed almost at once by Columbia (King's College), which took form in the years 1746–1754, and by the University of Pennsylvania, 1749–1756.

Benjamin Franklin was largely responsible for the founding of the University of Pennsylvania. Naturally, it was established on humanistic principles, since its founder was a thoroughgoing son of the Enlightenment. In the first Constitution of the University, of 1749, drafted by Franklin and the attorney-general, there was no mention of religion, the church or the ministry. The earlier colleges in the colonies, of course, had been established primarily for the purpose of preparing young men for the ministry, the "earlier congregations at least 'dreading to leave an illiterate ministry to the churches when our present ministers shall lie in the dust.'"[5]

The more formal purposes of the new institution were published in 1756, as the product, no doubt, of Dr. William Smith, the first provost, but done in the spirit of Franklin. Throughout is heard the "note of the modern spirit. The purpose is plainly to enrich and to enlarge the mind, and also to give to it efficiency."[6] The course of study was the most comprehensive in the colonies up to that time and included Latin, Greek, mathematics, metaphysics, logic, ethics, rhetoric, astronomy, botany, zoology, physics, and French. The Holy Bible was prescribed as a text, "to be read daily from the beginning, to supply the deficiencies of the whole. . . . When human science has done its utmost, and when we have thought the youth worthy of the honors of the Seminary, yet still we must recommend them to the *Scriptures of God*, in order to complete their wisdom, to regulate their conduct thro life, and guide them to happiness forever."[7] It was in this university in his own city that Neill spent his first two college years, entering in 1837 at the age of fourteen.

At the end of this period and just before leaving for Amherst, Edward Neill received a solicitous, devout, and affectionate letter from his mother on his sixteenth birthday:

My dear Edward

With this letter you will receive a watch presented to you with the affectionate love of your Father and Mother. It is my birthday and yours. I my dear boy am fast leaving these scenes; you are just entering them, and my beloved child it is a world where you will be very often tryed[sic], and tempted, but I beseech you, to hold fast your integrity; never do any thing your conscience tells you is wrong: You have been brought up to know right, and wrong, and my child, you have the daily prayers of your affectionate Father and Mother, that you may become a child of God. Oh! my child, think calmly and seriously of these things, they are not idle tales, but awful responsibilitys[sic], you are passing from childhood to manhood, your passions strong, think for yourself, act for yourself. Let no one persuade you to do, or say, any thing which your Saviour in heaven would condemn. With the watch I intended to give you a bible but your brother Henry had already done it. Oh! that I could prevail on you to read but one chapter a day with prayer, it will be one of the greatest comforts to your anxious Mother, and a lasting blessing to yourself. Pray nightly to your heavenly Father to bless you, in this world and in the world to come. Keep this letter my beloved child, and when I am in the silent grave, and the troubles and cares of a wicked world afflict you, read this letter, follow my advice, and think it is your dead Mother speaks. . . .[8]

Indeed, this was one of the few family letters that Neill cherished and preserved throughout his lifetime.

In the fall of 1839, young Neill transferred to Amherst College where, "crowning a hilltop, the college rises from the encircling plain like some castellated citadel. . . . To the north lies one of the loveliest village commons in New England."[9] His brother, Henry, had graduated from Amherst five years before, had a church in nearby Hatfield, and was to marry one of President Humphrey's five daughters in Edward's senior year, after the dignified and formal courtship of the period.

Neill was in college in a time of very great growth in higher education. Colleges in the United States multiplied rapidly up to the Civil War. There were 182 permanent colleges by 1861, and of these 131 were established between 1830 and 1861. Amherst College, opened in 1821 and chartered in 1825, was the forty-fourth of these colleges. The college of the period was "designed primarily as a 'nursery of ministers,' and was fostered as a 'child of the church.'"[10] The denominations were growing apace in these years due to a series of revivals that spread from the east to the frontier communities. This brought a "veritable 'Second Awakening' throughout the land."[11]

The colleges in Neill's youth were growing with the denominations and the prevailing institution of the period was the denominational college. This time of accelerated growth in higher education was also concomittant with the great western migrations. In fact, "the American college was typically a frontier institution. It was designed primarily to meet the needs of pioneer communities, and was established in most cases on the frontier line of settlement," as a result of which a distinctive American college evolved, "shaped and adapted to the peculiar needs of an advancing people." [12] Professor W. S. Tyler of Amherst College in 1856 said of the American colleges: "They are the people's colleges. . . . Scarcely anything in America is more distinctively American than the relation between the colleges and the common people." [13]

Amherst College, Neill's alma mater, came about as the result of the "irrepressible desire of residents of the Connecticut valley to have a college of their own." [14] It was distinctly a community enterprise. It was an outgrowth of Amherst Academy which was opened on December 5, 1814, for boys and girls. In 1821, there were 100 boys and 69 girls in attendance. In 1824, girls were excluded and the Academy became preparatory to the College.

Colonel Rufus Graves of Amherst, a great visionary, became a trustee of the Academy in 1816, and devoted himself without stint from that date to 1834 to the establishment and development of Amherst College. Associated with him were two other laymen, Squire H. Wright Strong and Samuel Fowler Dickinson. By May 19, 1819, the sum of $37,244 had been pledged or paid by 274 subscribers (The population of Amherst in 1820 was 1917). The cornerstone was laid on August 9, 1820. Dr. Zephaniah Swift Moore, president of Williams College, was elected president on May 8, 1821, and was inaugurated on September 18, 1821. One-half of the students of Williams College followed their beloved president and Amherst opened with fifty-three students in all four classes. The fifty-one year old president, who weighed 240 pounds, was to teach theology and moral philosophy, and was to receive a salary of $1200 with the "usual perquisites."

Neill came to a college that was founded to give gratuitous instruction to "indigent young men of promising talents and hopeful piety, who shall manifest a desire to obtain a liberal education with a sole view to the Christian Ministry."[15] Noah Webster, president of the board of trustees, said at the laying of the cornerstone in 1820: "This institution will grow and flourish, and become auxiliary to a thousand associations which Christian philanthropy has formed to reclaim and evangelize the miserable children of Adam."[16]

A distinguished early graduate of Amherst recalls that "the drive that brought the new college into being was inspired by the hope, expressed in an unusually candid letter by Noah Webster, that it would serve to counteract the errors disseminated from Cambridge. Amherst, in other words, was to be a citadel of Congregational orthodoxy against the lamentable Unitarian heresies of Harvard."[17]

Dr. Heman Humphrey, who was president of Amherst in Neill's time, had been elected on the death of President Moore, in 1823, and served until 1845, when he resigned. He was a graduate of Yale, where he had worked his entire way through school. He had had Congregational churches in Fairfield, Connecticut, and Pittsfield. He was famed as a revivalist. A much later successor, President C. M. Fuess, describes him as follows:

More frigidly intellectual than warmly emotional, conducted himself with coldness and reserve, and was bilious rather than sanguine in temperament. It was quickly evident, however, that he was not only a man of marked simplicity of character, humility of heart, and genuine practical wisdom, but also a person of excellent executive ability, with the farsightedness to form plans and the perseverance to carry them through. He was not clever or showy, and had no sparkling wit. His conscience was sensitive . . . was of medium height, with dark eyes, a full ruddy face, and a rather unusual fringe of black curly hair. He was especially interested in the cause of temperance . . . a zealous champion of orthodox, evangelistic religion, Christian Missions. . . .[18]

In 1825, the College received its Charter from the state. Two of the articles were unusual for the Christian colleges. They prescribed "that no Instructor in said College shall ever be required by the Trustees to profess any particular religious opinions, as a test of office; and no student shall be denied the privilege of said college on account of the religious opinions he may entertain."[19] This was remarkable in view of the strong orthodox Calvinistic beliefs of the founders.

Qualifications for admission were made the same as for Yale College, and the institution was patterned after Yale and Dartmouth, rather than Harvard with its Unitarianism. Indigent students to the number of twenty in the beginning were aided by the "Charity Fund," which amounted to $52,194 by November 21, 1822. In

1835, Edward Dickinson, probably the most distinguished citizen in the town and father of the poet, Emily Dickinson, became the treasurer of the College, serving to 1873. In 1836, the salaries of the instructors were increased to $1,000, and that of the president to $1,500.

The peak enrollment came in 1836–1837, with 259 students. In Neill's senior year, 1841–1842, the enrollment was 142 students, the decline coming because of student and alumni dissatisfaction with President Humphrey, who was a victim of circumstances. Board in the late 1830's was fifty per cent higher than at the opening of the College. In 1834, annual college expenses were $96 and they had risen to $150 in 1837. The College was severely affected by the panic of 1837. The debt of the College was $12,000 in 1839. Efforts for state appropriations were unsuccessful until 1845, when the legislature granted $25,000.

A very advanced curricular proposal was made by the faculty in 1826 on the grounds that the curriculum of American colleges was not "sufficiently modern and comprehensive." It was proposed to substitute French and German for Greek and Latin and to put a greater emphasis on modern history and science. In response to a request by the trustees for a plan, the faculty kept the classical course but presented a parallel course, with modern languages, and with greater prominence given to English literature, modern history, civil and political law, and physics and chemistry.[20] In 1826, eighteen of the sixty-seven freshmen elected this course, but due to differences, inadequate staff, and indifference, the course was abandoned in 1829 by the trustees.

Dr. Richard Salter Stores, of the class of 1839, long after described the curriculum of Neill's college generation:

> Latin and Greek, grammatically taught. Mathematics. More or less natural science as then understood. Something of philosophy. Something, no doubt, of instruction in ethics. We had moderate courses in rhetoric and logic, and a very slight smattering of French. We had no German, Italian, or Spanish; no history, very little, if anything, of political economy; no instruction in art; no leadership into the life of the Old World and the secrets of its renown, and no elective studies whatever.[21]

In Neill's day, the faculty included Nathan Welby Fiske in moral philosophy and physics; Ebenezer S. Snell in mathematics and natural philosophy; William Seymour Tyler in Greek and Latin; William Chauncey Fowler in rhetoric and oratory; and Edward Hitchcock, in chemistry and natural history, who became president in 1845.[22]

Religion was a matter of paramount concern in the College. There were two sermons on the Sabbath in the college church, and there was a religious lecture every Thursday evening. In 1832, morning prayers were set at 4:45 in the summer and at 5:45 in the winter. These and the first class were held before breakfast. Revivals were a normal periodic event. There were seven between 1823–1842, the sixth in the spring term of 1839, and the seventh in the summer term of 1842.

In the revival of 1839, there were twenty conversions and 111 of the 180 students were professing Christians. Neill did not confess conversion until shortly after he had left Amherst. The revivals were always followed by an increased interest in missions. In 1821 the "Theological Society" was formed, which grew into the "Society of Inquiry." There seems to have been a missionary society organized on July 14, 1828. It took the name of "Friends," and held its last meeting on July 14, 1841.[23] The "Missionary Band" was organized a few years later. An early alumnus noted that "it is not considered anything out of the way for even pious men to take a walk on Sunday, and it is the universal custom here." [24]

Literary societies were central in the extra-curricular life at Amherst. The Alexandrian and Athenian societies were founded at once in October, 1821, followed by the Social Union in 1827, as a secret society. Neill was a member of the latter. There was great rivalry between these societies. All had extensive libraries, the Athenians having 1172 volumes in 1828. *Horae Collegianae* was the excellent literary magazine in the years 1837–1841.

In 1837, Alpha Delta Phi was the first national secret society to be established at Amherst, followed in 1841 by the Gamma chapter of Psi Upsilon, of which Neill was one of the leading founders. Interest in the literary societies began to wane in the 1840's.

The faculty in 1842 made a formal demand for the constitution and records of both fraternities. The members refused, preferring to transfer to other colleges rather than break their oaths. Neill wrote a long letter to his brother Henry on December 10, 1841, vigorously presenting the case of the students and asking Henry to intercede on their behalf at Amherst. "As individuals," he wrote, "I have the greatest respect for all the faculty and even love for many of them; they have always treated me gentlemanly, kindly, forbearingly. But with regard to their power of governing I must say with all due respect I never saw such bad managers in my life." He went on to say that at least twenty students would leave the college if the faculty persisted in its inquiry, and that a student rebellion might occur. He quoted his own oration at the organization of the fraternity: " . . . *Our chapter* is to be preserved at *all hazards, all sacrifices*. . . . Our pledge to secrecy is Christian not Punic. . . . Let us be determined to carry into effect what we have commenced, quail before no man, no body of men. The righteousness of our cause should be our only thought: To God alone submit." He indicates he will leave Amherst and writes: "Pa has determined to send me back to Amherst; if I return the society must go on or I must be expelled." [25] Since some of the ablest students in the College were involved, the faculty let the matter drop. In the year after he graduated, Neill sent a gift of four busts to the fraternity. Only the one of Cicero arrived intact. The heads of Plato, Demosthenes, and one other, were "shockingly broken."

There was no college commons and the students ate in small groups at boarding houses. Their rooms were heated by wood fires in open fireplaces, each student furnishing his own wood. Water for washing was carried upstairs from the college well behind the chapel. There was an outdoor gymnasium, with a circular running track, and some home-made apparatus. Daily wear was pretty formal. "The young gentlemen of the College sported frock coats with a keen consciousness of their new dignity."[26] "There was a fairly incessant flow of frolic and banter and some horseplay. . . . For feminine society there were two resources: the young ladies of the village and the inmates of Mount Holyoke Female Seminary at South Hadley, ten miles away."[27]

There were twenty-eight graduates in Neill's class in 1842. The Society of Alumni was organized in that year. In Henry Ward Beecher's class of forty in 1834, eighteen became clergymen, nine teachers, five lawyers, four doctors, and four businessmen. The spirit of worldliness began seeping in around 1835. From the class of forty-two men in 1854, eleven became ministers, twelve lawyers, nine businessmen, five teachers, and five physicians. President Humphrey estimated that by 1845, of approximately 765 graduates, at least four hundred were in the ministry or preparing for it. In those days, most of the ministerial students went on to Andover Theological Seminary, the "citadel of Calvinistic orthodoxy in New England."[28]

Young Neill was but nineteen when he graduated from Amherst. His life plans were undecided. His father wrote to him on June 8, 1842, revealing that they had been considering mostly the mercantile business. The father approved this since "it affords a fine field for honorable exertion, and to do good to our fellow men provided we are governed in our efforts by the principles of the Gospel and are not carried away by the selfish principle." He went on to express the hope of the mother and father that God would open Edward's heart to conversion. "If that blessed event should take place we should then beg you to direct your thoughts to the Gospel Ministry, that is the greatest business on this earth for a poor Mortal-immortal to be engaged in, that is a business in which he cannot fail if his heart is right with God." [29] The father concluded by saying that Mr. William Welsh had mentioned a probable vacancy in his counting house in the next month.

Edward was converted by the following spring and had joined the family church. At that time he was considering a commission in the United States Marine Corps, and his father informed him of an opening in the Iron Works of T. A. Spencer as a clerk at $150 a year, with board and washing. Edward, under the compulsion of his recent religious experience, decided to enter Andover Seminary, where he was a student in 1843–44.

Andover Seminary was opened on September 28, 1808, as the first theological school in New England, as a response to the cultural and spiritual conflicts of those decades, and as a part of the "Evangelical Reawakening." It was the answer of orthodox Calvinism to the rationalism, Arminianism, Universalism, and Unitarianism of the day, brought to an alarming challenge in 1805 when Harvard went over to Unitarianism.[30] The seminary was built "sturdily to breast the gales that beat against Puritan orthodoxy, as Brick Row on Andover

Hill fronted the northern blasts that in winter sweep unchecked from the far Laurentian highlands in Canada. The halls of the Seminary were permeated by a theology as cold and as irresistible."[31]

A generation before Neill went to Andover there were two groups of Calvinists in New England: the followers of Samuel Hopkins, representing High, or Consistent, Calvinism, and the Old Calvinists. In about 1806 each group was considering establishing a seminary. The Andover group of Old Calvinists founded theirs on September 2, 1807, and the other group was persuaded to unite with them. In the first years the faculty had a Hopkinsean leaning. Funds were furnished by descendants of John Phillips, founder of Phillips Academy in Andover, and by Samuel Abbott, an Andover businessman.

The Founders expressed their purpose in the constitution to increase "the number of learned and able defenders of the Gospel of Christ, as well as of orthodox, pious, and zealous ministers of the New Testament; being moved, as we hope, by a principle of gratitude to God and benevolence to man."[32] The Founders earnestly believed that they were defending the truth of God against evil and error. Their basic problem was to change men from the state of sin to that of holiness. Although this change of man's heart was a matter of supernatural election, they felt that the work of the preacher and of the church was very relevant. The conservatism and dogmatism of these Calvinists prompted the Unitarians to call Andover Seminary "an institution which would have disgraced the bigotry of the Middle Ages." [33]

The Founders did everything possible to keep heresy out of the Seminary and to safeguard the students from error. The annual public examinations of the students were designed to this end. The professors and students "alike felt themselves anointed kings and priests, with a momentous task to perform for the world." [34] Naturally, the Seminary emphasized the two movements of revivalism and missions, which stemmed from the central emphasis on conversion.

In Neill's day, the first year of the three-year course was given mainly to the study of the Scriptures, the second to systematic theology, and the third was divided between Ecclesiastical History and Sacred Rhetoric, with exegetical studies in all three years.[35] Students of any Protestant denomination were acceptable. Every applicant had to be "regularly educated at some respectable College or University, or has otherwise made literary acquisitions which, as preparatory to theological studies are substantially equivalent to a liberal education, and that he sustains a fair moral character, is of a prudent and discreet deportment, and is hopefully possessed of personal piety." [36] Each applicant was then examined by the faculty as to his personal piety, his object in pursuing theological studies, and his knowledge of the "learned languages."

In 1844 the number of students fell below one hundred and remained in the nineties for several years. In the first half century of the Seminary, Dartmouth sent

358 of its graduates to the Seminary, Amherst 326, Yale 314, Middlebury 195, Williams 153, Bowdoin 108, Brown 78, and Harvard 75. The newer western colleges were represented by Marietta with eighteen, Oberlin sixteen, Knox four, Wabash three, Iowa College three, Beloit two, and Centre two students. Of the total, 129 were not college graduates.

The professors in Neill's day were Leonard Woods in Christian Theology; Moses Stuart in Sacred Literature; Edwards Amos Park in Sacred Rhetoric; Ralph Emerson in Ecclesiastical History; and Bela Bates Edwards in Hebrew Language and Literature. A more liberal and critical spirit developed after the mid-thirties, somewhat in tune with the vast political, social, economic and intellectual changes taking place in New England and in the nation. Moses Stuart, "the father of biblical learning in America,"[37] and Edwards A. Park were the principal figures in a trend that was strongly resisted. In fact, Andover stood staunchly against the main currents until 1881, when it became the champion of evangelical religious liberalism, with its new *Andover Review* (1883) as the principal organ of theological reconstruction.

Religion was the diet of the students, in and out of the classrooms. The Seminary had its own Chapel and Sunday preaching by the faculty members. The Society of Inquiry was for the study of missions. On one Monday each month there was the "Monthly Concert of Prayer for Foreign Missions." On Wednesday evenings professors and students discussed religion informally in a general "conference." The "Porter Rhetorical" programs on Thursday evenings were a secular interlude. The "Jews Meeting" took place on Friday evenings at the home of Professor Porter for the purpose of praying for the conversion of the Jews. A social prayer meeting was held on Saturday nights in the lower lecture room of the Chapel. Yearly fast days were observed to increase pious devotion.

During the time Neill was at Andover, twelve men of the class of '43 developed the custom of meeting in the Library by moonlight for prayer. The spiritual needs of the settlers on the frontier rested heavily upon their hearts. They decided on a cooperative venture in Iowa and eleven of the group decided to go. This was the famous Iowa Band.[38]

The Seminary disregarded public matters and politics until slavery became an unavoidable issue. Professor B. B. Edwards then founded the American Society for the Amelioration of the Condition of Slaves, and a small abolition society was formed. President Justin Edwards was the first agent of the American Temperance Society.

The students lived a life of "spartan simplicity," even in Neill's day. At the beginning there was no tuition, rent was nominal, and board in Commons was cheap. Indigent students were assisted with about half of their expenses. The students made wheelbarrows and coffins in the carpenter shop, the latter serving as "grim reminders of the brevity of life." [39] The climax of the year came in the "anniversaries" when every class was examined publicly before the Trustees, visitors, faculty, and public, who packed Bartlet Chapel.

Neill found himself in an institution whose impact and outreach through its graduates was very impressive. In the first ten years of the life of the American Board, all but one of the missionaries it sent out were Andover men. In thirty-eight years, one hundred Andover graduates were on the mission field. Andover men brought about the organization of the American Home Mission Society in 1826, and formed the Iowa Band in 1843 which "marked a beginning of a new growth of Congregationalism in the West."[40] Class after class sent its quota westward. Only one class was unrepresented up to 1856. The classes of 1825 and 1829 sent twenty-three each, and those of 1832 and 1843 sent twenty each. In 1859 it was reported that of more than 2000 students who had studied at Andover, 250 had been or were ministers or missionaries west of the state of New York.[41] One of these, of course, was Edward Neill. In the West, most of the Congregationalists assumed Presbyterian church relations.

Neill found his year at Andover tough going. In a letter to his father on January 24, 1844, he bewailed his difficulties in concentrating on his studies, and remarked: "The truth is I went to College too early in life, my mind was not sufficiently mature to know anything about the studies of the Senior year and I now reap the effects of my inattention." He suggested that he stay out a year and discipline himself by teaching. "I am too young," he continued, "too indisciplined – I have written just what I believe and just what I thought I ought to write on this point. I am anxious to be a useful minister and to be one I must not be in a hurry."[42]

His decision to go into the ministry remained firm.

> The more my attention is turned to the ministerial office, the more do I feel that I would not be performing the duty I owe to my God if I should attempt any other avocation. Though I feel I have but little talent and no power of extemporaneous discourse and no ability to lead . . . public worship, still I am confident that if my heart is right, places though they may be in the wilderness and in swamps will be found in which I may do good to mortals with immortal souls.

His letter concluded on a typical and timeless student theme: "About the middle of March it will probably be necessary for me to ask for more of the 'filthy lucre.' . . . My love to Ma – it would do my soul good to receive a short line from her."

Neill did teach for part of a year in 1846, in Accomack County, Virginia. His father had died on October 7, 1845. Neill began to have doubts about the ministry and his Philadelphia pastor, Rev. Albert Barnes, tactfully tried to persuade him that he had the qualifications for the "inestimable privilege" of preaching the gospel.

In Virginia, Neill was brought squarely up against the matter of slavery. A Mr. Hargis, a Methodist pastor in Guilford, had evidently been torn from his pulpit by outsiders because he had expressed his convictions on the issue. Neill defended the right of Hargis, whom he called an "imprudent and rough man," to preach whatever doctrines he would so long as his congregation wanted to hear him. "Admit the principle," he wrote, "that a world has the right to decide what doctrines of a preacher are dangerous and that moment you open the door for the destruction of God's temples throughout the land. The only safe principle is that every body of Christians however small has a right to employ whatsoever religious teacher they please and not what pleases the world." [43] He called upon the Constitution of Virginia for support.

In this "Minute" of a conversation with Robert J. Poulson on November 2, 1846, regarding slavery, Neill advocated a "safe mean between Abolition and Pro-Slavery principles." In reply to the question "If I thought the liberation of slaves under any circumstances desirable," Neill replied "that if any plan could be devised by the South itself by which the slave could be liberated and the interests of the owner not be jeopardized . . . I would be heartily in favor of it." For this, Poulson called him an Abolitionist.

Neill resigned his teaching position on December 5, 1846, in a letter to T. P. Bogwell, effective on December 24, as a protest to the attack of the "lawyers and some of the other principal men of the County arrayed against one of the oldest and most useful religious denominations on the Eastern shore. . . . An attack has been made on the religious liberties of Virginia." He concluded, "I must leave the county and seek a place of residence where such opinions are not deemed heretical and where ministers are not dragged out of the Pulpit while in the peaceful discharge of their duties." [44]

Neill proceeded to complete his theological studies under his pastor and mentor, Rev. Albert Barnes, and Dr. Thomas Brainerd of Philadelphia. Still undecided, discouraged, and in debt, he was in Geneseo, Illinois, in June, 1847, evidently to explore life and work in the West. His sister, Emily, wrote to him on June 8:

> Don't be faint-hearted. . . . I would labor to pay my debts. . . . Give up the idea of preaching if you cannot do so without incuring[sic] expense. It is better for you not to preach until you are released from your pecuniary difficulties. As to your being married you must not think of it until you have paid your debts. . . . Write ev'rything in your letters – I do not care how blue they are – it does one good – to be able to blow out – and sigh out too. . . . If in the next letter you tell me that you are a tender of an engine on a steamboat, a teamster, a collier – I shall shout for joy – you will make a man yet. . . .[45]

In a letter ten days later, Emily rejoiced that Neill had resolved finally to preach. He was then licensed by the Presbytery of Galena.

In October, Neill returned East to marry Nancy, daughter of Richard Hall, of Snow Hill, whom he commended forty years later as a "true wife who has lightened the home, and is beloved by the community in which she lives."[46] She bore him five children.

"Having decided to identify himself," as he put it, "with frontier communities, that had not been molded into form,"[47] he was sent with his bride as a home missionary to preach to the lead miners at Elizabeth, a hamlet near Galena in Illinois. In the spring of 1848 he was ordained. The restless, eager young preacher was not satisfied. He records of himself:

> Having learned that steps had been taken to ask Congress to form a new territory, north of Iowa, and like the Apostle Paul, not wishing to build on another man's foundation, he wrote, in October, 1848, to the Rev. A. Kent, the senior member of the Presbytery: "I do not know what your arrangements may be about the supply of that distant field, but, if you can fill my present post, I am ready to go as the pioneer in that region. My wife and I are contented enough here, but it is almost too civilized. The latter fact would make it desirable to some that would not like to go so far from the luxuries and comforts of the East. If then, you are of the opinion that I and mine are the persons suited for a new field, I am at your disposal." [48]

Early in 1849, the Presbytery of Galena granted the permission desired, to the Neills. The Home Mission Board commissioned him to labor in the Territory of Minnesota (established on April 9, 1849).[49] Neill attended the General Assembly of the Presbyterian Church in Philadelphia shortly after taking his new post. While there he collected funds from relatives and friends to erect a church in the hamlet of St. Paul.

The Neills arrived in St. Paul by boat on April 23rd. At twenty-six, Edward Neill had at least found the locale of his life's work. He had finally arrived at man's estate in a vigorous frontier community.

Neill and Pioneer Schools

Neill and Pioneer Schools

WHAT kind of pioneer community was it to which Neill came in 1849? Rev. Albert Barnes, his spiritual guide, in a well-informed and eloquent sermon on behalf of the American Home Missionary Society, preached in New York and Philadelphia in May, 1849, describing a tour in the West, said:

I visited the Falls of St. Anthony . . . [where] I had views of the greatness of my country such as I have never had in the crowded capitols and the smiling villages of the East. . . . You ascend the Mississippi amid scenery unsurpassed in beauty probably in the world. . . . God who did all this, that we might prepare it for the abode of a civilized and Christian people.[1]

The new Territory of Minnesota had a population of less than five thousand in 1849. By mid-summer St. Paul had a population of 910, Stillwater 609, and St. Anthony 248. Edward Neill reported that St. Paul was "just emerging from a collection of Indian whiskey shops, and birch-roofed cabins of half-breed voyageurs."[2]

In a popular article in *Graham's Magazine* in 1855, Neill summarized the growth of the bustling town:

The origin of the settlement is ignoble . . . It became a choice spot for those modern harpies, the frontier whiskey sellers, to pitch their tents. . . . In the year 1847 there were about one hundred persons dwelling here, chiefly half breeds; but at the time of the formation of the territory, in 1849, several American families had moved here, and the population was about three hundred.

The close of the year 1853 discovers but few of the original tenements or settlers, but in their places modern and tasteful mansions, and an active, intelligent population of about four thousand five hundred.

Saint Paul is a city of three hills or plateaus, overlooking the Mississippi, and in the rear surrounded by a gracefully undulating and elevated ridge, already covered with cottages, and destined to afford sites for many more handsome suburban residences. The central plateau is about ninety feet above the water, but descends gradually, forming a good steamboat landing at such extremity. This may be termed the city proper.

The plain from the river to the semicircular ridge in the rear is about one mile in width, and until quite recently was a dense grove. Upon it stands at present the First and Second Presbyterian, Methodist, Episcopal, and Roman Catholic Churches, the Stone Hospital of the Sisters of Mercy, the Town Hall, the Court House, the Territorial Capitol, and the Baldwin School.[3]

Neill concluded the article with a prophetic comment on the town that was to become Minneapolis: "Upon the eastern shore of the Mississippi, opposite to Hennepin and Nicollet and Spirit Islands, is the town of Saint Anthony, which has all the appearance of an enterprising and intelligent New England village. This village must be a place of importance."

Fredrika Bremer, the distinguished Swedish author who visited the Territory in 1850, exulted, "This Minnesota is a glorious country," and concluded prophetically, "just the country for Northern emigrants; just the country for a new Scandinavia. . . . What a glorious new Scandinavia might not Minnesota become."[4]

Growth and activity in St. Paul in 1849 were almost unbelievable. The American Fur Company moved its headquarters from Mendota to the teeming town. Most of the leading citizens of the place were partners or ex-partners in the fur company: Henry H. Sibley, Henry M. Rice, Dr. Charles W. Borup, Charles H. Oakes, Norman W. Kittson, and Martin McLeod. A summer traveler reported that there were two good hotels, that two-thirds of the houses had been built in that year, that "gaming is quite prevalent," "a good school is kept here," that there were resident Roman Catholic, Presbyterian, Baptist, and Methodist ministers, and a visiting Episcopal clergyman, and a log church of the Catholics, with services in French.[5] Seventy-five buildings were built in May. The three-story American House, owned by Henry M. Rice, was built in ten weeks. There were seven contractors in town. Lots were selling for twenty-five to five hundred dollars and land outside the town at from ten to one hundred dollars an acre. The farmers already established were for the most part French.

The winter of 1848–49 had been one of the most severe in years, with the usual temperature between twenty-five and thirty degrees below zero. As a result, the first boat had not arrived until April 9, always an exciting event, particularly when the Sioux Indians filled the town. The beautiful trip from Galena took a little more than three days for the round trip and cost six dollars for one way.[6] In 1848, the one overland route to the outside had been opened, crossing into Wisconsin at Stillwater and extending from there to Galena. A mail and stage line was established. The stage line between St. Paul and Stillwater ran three times weekly, in each direction.

Neill had arrived on one of the earliest boats, on April 23, and he preached his first sermon in the log school house on Bench Street on Sunday the twenty-ninth. In the summer of 1849 he held regular services in the Central House. In September his frame church was completed, largely paid for by members of his family church, the First Presbyterian Church of Philadelphia.[7]

In the meantime Henry Sibley had gone to Washington as delegate to Congress from the Territory. The distinguished Alexander Ramsey[8] had arrived to take up his duties as Governor of the Territory. Fredrika Bremer was a guest in his home in 1850 and recorded that "the drawing room at Governor Ramsey's house is also his office, and Indians and work people, and ladies and gentlemen, all are alike admitted."[9] She noted that he was building a spacious new home outside the town on a hill.

During the year 1849 the first Masonic Lodge was founded, the first brickhouse in St. Paul was erected by Neill for his residence at the corner of Fourth and Washington Streets, and the First Presbyterian Church was built of wood, by Neill on the lot adjoining his home. Both lots were given by Henry M. Rice. The first town pump was erected at Jackson and Third Streets. The Sons of Temperance were organized on May 9th. The Fourth of July was celebrated with a parade, and two hundred persons banqueted in the evening at the American House. In October Indians shipped out two thousand barrels of cranberries.

James M. Goodhue, a native of New Hampshire, a fellow alumnus of Amherst with Neill, and a lawyer by profession who had published a newspaper in Wisconsin, arrived in St. Paul in mid-April, 1849, with his press.[10] He brought out the first issue of the *Minnesota Pioneer*, the first paper in the Territory, on April 28th. In this issue the newcomer editorialized, "a more beautiful site for a town cannot be imagined." This weekly paper, under the very enlightened editorship of Goodhue, was originally neutral in politics, cost two dollars a year in advance, and came out under the slogan, "Sound Principles, Safe Men and Moderate Measures." The Whig *Minnesota Chronicle*, edited by J. Hughes, appeared on May 31, and in July came the *Minnesota Register* with N. McLean and J. Owens at the masthead. These two papers were united in October. The *Minnesota Pioneer* became Democratic and a vigorous political rivalry developed between the two papers.

The hotels and boarding houses were crowded in 1849. Board cost one dollar a day and from two dollars and a half to five dollars a week. The *Minnesota Pioneer* warned in its very first issue: "We advise settlers who are swarming into St. Paul in such multitudes, to bring along tents and bedding, to provide for their comfort until they can build houses, as it *is utterly impossible* to hire a building." Neill records that in April he had roomed with Mr. Lott Moffett in an unfinished house in which some boarders had to sleep on the floor. He slept with a Mr. Baldwin on a buffalo robe placed on a rough home-made bed-stead.[11] A visitor in May reported staying in a boarding house "consisting of one room, about sixteen feet square, in which sixteen persons, including men, women, and children, contrived to lodge."[12]

The first church in St. Paul was the Roman Catholic log chapel of St. Paul built by Rev. Lucien Galtier on Bench Street in October, 1841, and served by him until 1844. Father Augustine Ravoux served the St. Paul and Mendota parishes until 1851, when Bishop Joseph Cretin came.[13] Samuel Spates and his wife were Methodist missionaries to the Chippewas from 1839 to 1855, and Chauncey Hobart was appointed in 1849 to superintend the Methodist work with the whites in the St. Paul and Minnesota district. Rev. T. S. Williamson, M. D., was an evangelistic and medical Presbyterian missionary to the Dakotas at Kaposia, three miles down the river from St. Paul.

Neill gave the invocation when the Territorial legislature assembled for the first time on September 3, 1849, in rooms in the Central House, at the corner of Bench and Minnesota Streets, overlooking the river. A flag was run up in front of the hotel in the presence of the town folks and some blanketed Indians. Governor Ramsey read his message on the next day.

In this message, Governor Ramsey urged that attention be given to the schools and to education. Congress by the Organic Act of March 3, 1849, had granted the Territory two sections – the sixteenth and thirty-sixth – in each township for its public schools. The Council and the House of Representatives each appointed a Committee on Schools. These turned in able reports. G. H. Pond was chairman of the House Committee, and Martin McLeod of the Committee in the Council.

McLeod was a native of Montreal, a fur trader and a scholar, who served in four legislatures. The statesmanlike Bill that he presented with the Committee's Report, became law on November 1, 1849. "With the name of this enlightened legislator," writes William W. Folwell, "who laid the foundation of a comprehensive school system must be associated that of the Reverend Edward D. Neill . . . who was doubtless his adviser."[14]

The McLeod Report has a timeless character in a democracy.

> The appointment of a committee on schools . . . is a recognition of the principle that the general diffusion of education, intellectual and moral, is essential to our present happy form of government, and that virtue and intelligence are the only pillars on which republican governments can safely rest; and every attempt to build up free institutions without these must ultimately fail. . . .
>
> Where all should be made to bear a part of the burthen, they, of course, should be admitted to an equal participation of the benefits, and all invidious distinctions be at once and forever abolished.
>
> The three great departments of education are physical, intellectual and moral. . . . Man should be educated for eternity, and fitted to take his place among those whose employment it will doubtless be to diffuse happiness throughout that sphere in which their Creator destined them to move. No system of education, then, can be complete or desirable, which does not view man in this light.

Morality and religion should be regarded as the most essential elements of education, and should hold their due prominence in every institution of learning . . . and bigotry, fanaticism, and narrow-minded sectarian prejudice, alike be for ever excluded from every temple of knowledge.[15]

McLeod spoke particularly of the desirability of establishing high schools and academies.

The Act as passed was "to establish and maintain common schools . . . for the education of all the children and youth of the Territory." A territorial tax of one-fourth of one percent was authorized and this might be supplemented when necessary by a tax to be voted in each district. Every township with not less than five families was to be a school district. Three trustees were to be chosen for each district and these were to examine and appoint teachers.

Neill discovered that there were a few schools in the region when he came to St. Paul. The first schools in what became the Territory of Minnesota were mission schools. The Roman Catholics established a mission and school in 1818 at Pembina on the Red River (which was a part of the Territory of Minnesota later but became a part of Dakota when Minnesota became a state). They also established a mission school in 1838 at Grand Portage, a great fur center on the peninsula between the Pigeon River and Lake Superior.[16] The first Protestant mission school was established at Sandy Lake in 1832 by Frederick Ayer, of Massachusetts, the son of a Presbyterian minister. Various other mission schools for the Indians were organized subsequent to this. Mrs. Matilda

ST. PAUL IN 1853

[From a lithograph in Isaac I. Stevens, *Report of Explorations for a Pacific Railway*, 53].

MAIDEN'S ROCK — LAKE PEPIN

[From a photograph of a water color by Edwin J. Whitefield made in 1858, in a volume of original water colors by Whitefield (London, 1859), owned by the Minnesota Historical Society.]

Rumsey is credited with having taught the first school in the tiny village of St. Paul, for a brief time in 1845.[17] There was a school at Fort Snelling as early as 1823.

Miss Harriet Bishop was the first pioneer teacher of a regular school in St. Paul. She came to St. Paul in 1847 under the auspices of the National Popular Education Society, which had just been established on April 7, in Cleveland, to supply the western settlements with competent women teachers. All of the evangelical denominations united in the enterprise, of which ex-Governor William Slade of Vermont was the general agent and corresponding secretary. A letter came to the Society from Rev. Thomas S. Williamson, at Kaposia, urging that a teacher be sent to open a school in that village, where there were thirty-six children of school age, in a population that was half French. Harriet Bishop volunteered for this post.

This sturdy woman was a native of Vermont (born January 1, 1818), who had taught in the state of New York, and was studying under Miss Catherine Beecher at the New York State Normal School in Albany, when her opportunity came. She arrived in St. Paul on July 10, 1847, and nine days later opened her school in a mud-chinked cabin, ten by twelve feet, with a bark roof, three windows, and a very low door, located at what became Third and St. Peter. The cabin had once been used as a stable, and then as a blacksmith shop. The school opened with nine children, of whom two were white. The number soon increased to forty, of whom eight were white. The new teacher at once started a

Sunday School that grew steadily. In 1849, the school moved to a "small frame building on the bluff, near the lower landing," at what is now the foot of Jackson Street.[18]

The Society sent Miss Amanda Hosford to Stillwater in 1848. In May, 1849, William Slade came to St. Paul with two more teachers. Miss Mary Scofield joined Harriet Bishop, and Miss Backus was sent to St. Anthony. Slade addressed the citizens of St. Paul in the school house on education on May 27th. Mr. Chauncey Hobart, the Methodist pastor, taught a boys' school in 1849 in the basement of the Methodist Church. In July, 1850, Mr. A. J. Baker opened a school in St. Paul. The attendance in his school soon grew from forty to eighty-five. Four Sisters of St. Joseph arrived in the town on November 2, 1851, to open their first school in the old Chapel of St. Paul.

Public schools were an immediate concern of the residents of the town. Neill was very active in their promotion. On December 1, 1849, shortly after the territorial legislature had passed the Common School Law, the citizens of St. Paul met and appointed a Provisional Committee on Schools. This was the first public school meeting on record in Minnesota. The Committee was composed of William H. Forbes, chairman, Edmund Rice, Rev. Mr. Hoyt, Rev. Mr. Parsons, and Rev. Mr. Neill. The Committee arranged to open three schools. It assumed the debt on the schools taught by Miss Bishop and Miss Scofield and appointed these women as teachers. The third teacher was Mr. Chauncey Hobart. Their remuneration was fixed at three dollars per pupil for a quarter of sixty days.

Neill found that there was an army post near St. Paul. A fort had been laid out by Colonel Henry Leavenworth at the confluence of the Minnesota and Mississippi Rivers in 1819. It was called Fort St. Anthony. Colonel Josiah Snelling relieved Leavenworth in 1820, and laid the cornerstone of the fort on September 10, 1820. In 1824 the name of the fort was changed to Fort Snelling.[19] Colonel G. A. Loomis assumed command in 1849. He frequently invited the ministers of the town to occupy the pulpit in the little chapel, where Dr. E. G. Gears, the Chaplain, usually preached. Neill was a great favorite with the officers and men of the old Sixth Infantry.[20] The *Minnesota Pioneer*, in its issue of Thursday, August 23, 1849, reported an illuminating episode:

> On Sunday last, the Rev. Mr. Neill and lady of St. Paul, were overturned in a buggy, in driving down the hill from this side of the ferry at Fort Snelling; but were providentially only slightly injured. The same day, a soldier from the fort, named Robert Downing, was going down the same hill with a cask of whiskey on his shoulder, fell down, and the cask falling upon him, broke three of his ribs, his thigh and his spine; so that he soon died – an awful commentary upon the text, that "the way of the transgressor is hard."

With a fitting sense of history and destiny, the Minnesota Historical Society was incorporated on October 20, 1849, on the initiative of Charles K. Smith, the Secretary of the Territory. Neill was a charter member and served as secretary for twelve years. He gave the first lecture of the Society on January 1, 1850, in the Methodist Church, on the French *Voyageurs* to the territory in the seventeenth century. The *Minnesota Pioneer* on the following day reported the address "which was not merely instructive but thrillingly eloquent. . . . One could seem to see actualy stirring before him, all the events described." In its issue of February 13, it published the address in full on the first and second pages of the paper. The Fort Snelling band had furnished music at the first meeting of the Society.

Neill, in a prophetic charge in his introduction, said: "You have been organized at a most favorable period. On the bluff where we are assembled, there are temples of religion and education, the indubitable marks of the Anglo-Saxon tread; yet around us, the skin-lodges of the Dakotas are still visible. . . . Prosecute then the objects for which the Society was incorporated, with vigor, 'Write your history as you go along,' and you will confer a favor upon the future inhabitants of Minnesota, for which they will be ever grateful."

A newcomer to Minnesota reported in 1850 that now St. Paul had six churches, twenty-five stores, six taverns, "groceries and gambling houses too numerous to mention," about fifty lawyers and land agents, two hundred and fifty gamblers, and "that Governor Ramsey owns a great quantity of land." [21] Patent medicines were popular and spirituous liquors flowed freely.[22] In March, a dog train of express mail arrived from the Pembina and Selkirk Settlements on the Red River, a distance of five hundred miles, covered in eighteen days. An Indian Council was held at Fort Snelling on June 11–12, between the Chippewas and the Sioux, to discuss the Treaty of 1843. Governor Ramsey presided.

In January, 1850, Neill organized the First Presbyterian Church, an event which the *Minnesota Pioneer* reported on January 9:

The First Presbyterian Church of St. Paul, was organized last Sunday, in the Rev. Neill's chapel. Bros. Selby and Tinker, who had before been chosen elders, were ordained by the laying on of hands, etc.
After the usual services of the forenoon there was a communion season. Rev. Dr. Williamson of the Little Crow Mission, was present, with several of the native Sioux, who are communicants of his church. The Dr. made some very affecting remarks, both in English, and in Sioux, alluding to this interesting union of Communionists of different colors and races, in which all believers in Christ were then invited to unite. . . . May this new branch from the banyan tree of the Church, take root in the Rock of Ages.

The frame chapel burned in May, 1850, and Neill immediately began the erection of a brick church at Third and St. Peter. This church contained the first large church bell in St. Paul and the first large pipe organ in Minnesota. The bell cost $205 and thirty-one local persons subscribed $121.18 to it, including ten dollars each from Henry H. Sibley and Henry M. Rice. The *Minnesota Pioneer* reported the opening of the new church in its issue of November 14:

Sunday Morning — what delightful, balmy sunshine! The Yankee left at about church time for below, but the Nominee lies devotionally at the Upper Landing, while the new church bell sends out its new, glorious peals, awakening holy associations on the east side of the river, and savage astonishment on the west side. All Saint Paul and the Nominee were at Mr. Neill's new church, where that energetic man, who has been sleepless in his efforts to accomplish the erection of this noble building, from the hour when his chapel was burnt down, on the 16th of last May – delivered an appropriate discourse, of which it is sufficient to say, that it was worthy of the occasion and of himself.

The Episcopal Church was being built at the same time, in the rear of the Library. A Baptist Church was organized on December 29, with twelve members. Neill aided in founding the Presbytery of Minnesota in 1850. In 1854, the First Presbyterian Church was enlarged and forty pews were added. In December of that year Neill resigned as minister of that church to become minister-at-large in St. Paul, in order to devote more time to education. On December 25, 1855, he organized the House of Hope Church.[23]

Alexander Ramsey had a specific recommendation on education in his message to the second Legislative Assembly on January 7, 1851:

The principle that society is bound to provide for its members *education*, as well as protection, is one of the most important that belongs to modern philosophy. . . . If there be any feature more distinct, more prominent, and more observable in the social structure of this great nation, than any other, it is the imperative obligation which rests on every community, to provide free elementary instruction for all its youth. . . .

To insure method and uniformity I would suggest the creation of the office of Superintendent of Schools. This officer could collect statistics, superintend the introduction of a proper and uniform series of textbooks, supervise the organization of schools, annually report to the Legislature the result of each year's operation.[24]

The Governor also recommended that the Legislature memorialize Congress for a grant of 100,000 acres to endow the University of Minnesota, in order to "secure a fair proportion of choice lands." The Legislative Assembly proceeded to enact legislation establishing the office of Superintendent of Schools, establishing the University of Minnesota at the Falls of St. Anthony, and memorializing Congress as suggested by the Governor. It was eighteen years, however, before collegiate work was begun in the university. Neill was chosen first Superintendent of Schools and he served from March, 1851, to June, 1853, for an honorarium of one hundred dollars a year.

Neill presented his first annual report to the Council on January 20, 1852. In his own Report as chairman of the Committee on Schools, Martin McLeod said "It is the first report issued by a Superintendent since the organization of the Territory, and is in many respects not only highly interesting, but valuable as a record for future reference, when Minnesota will number her schools by thousands."

Neill's report contained an excellent statistical picture of the schools in the territory. The Superintendent urged the establishment of grammar schools for the older and more advanced children in towns having more than one school district. He called attention to the need to build better school houses and make their surroundings attractive, and he urged uniformity in the selection of textbooks as against special preferences of teachers and citizens, and in spite of the importunities of publishers and booksellers.

In this very practical and statesmanlike report, one reads:

It is strange that "fathers who know how to give good gifts to their children," almost invariably neglect to furnish their offspring with a school house that is calculated to make the associations with their studies pleasant, or to teach them the principles of correct architecture, or give them a single idea of beauty. . . .

To make a full man, the boy must be developed physically as well as intellectually; and the village who would have its youth prosper most in school hours, should take care in this new country, where land is not held at an exorbitant price, that the school house be situated in the centre of at least an acre lot. Nothing raises a population so much in the estimation of a traveler, or emigrant, as to see a crowd of boys issuing from a pleasant school house, to play during the recess, upon a capacious lawn. . . .

The vocation of teacher is a noble one. He is far from being a drone in society, but is eminently one of the class of producers. His duties are such as often to require "an angel's wisdom."

The Superintendent has aimed to select such Reading Books,[25] as will be unobjectionable to any of the various classes of citizens. A fruitful source of difficulty in our Public Schools, has been the reading of lessons from the Protestant version of the Bible. It is believed that upon examination, there will be found no extracts in the Reading Books recommended, calculated to arouse any religious prejudice. If the state ever expects to have her schools receive the support of the *entire community*, those who have charge of public instruction cannot be too careful in excluding works that have a sectarian bias; and the "good" of every shade of religious belief, should watch that no instruction of that description be instilled by the teachers. . . .[26]

In 1852, permissive legislation was passed to establish public high schools.

In his second annual report, Neill summarized the history of education in Minnesota. He urged that schools be erected and used as schools for six days in the week and as churches on the seventh, rather than for religious zealots to rush in and solicit funds for a particular denomination at a time when there was neither a suitable school nor a common place of worship. He suggested that Protestants and Catholics could share the use of such buildings. He called attention to the fact that some teachers remained unpaid although there was ample provision for funds from taxation, and he urged that the office of County and School Treasurer be separated. In an appendix, he gave the School Law, with the Amendments of 1852, which included:

Sec. 2. For the better support of common schools and the general diffusion of education, there shall be set apart in the county treasurer, twenty-five per cent of all moneys paid into the county treasury, arising from the sale of spirituous or other liquors, and the proceeds of all fines for a breach of any penal laws of this territory, not otherwise appropriated by law.[27]

The regents of the University of Minnesota met for the first time on May 31, 1851, in the St. Charles Hotel in St. Anthony. They were Franklin Steele, President,

Isaac Atwater, Secretary, J. W. North, Treasurer, William R. Marshall, Librarian, H. H. Sibley, B. B. Meeker, A. Van Vorhes, and C. K. Smith. They decided to establish a Preparatory Department and to solicit funds for it. The school was to be erected on four acres of ground offered by Franklin Steele, near the center of St. Anthony, on the bluff just above the mills, facing Main Street and the river. The cost was to be limited to $2,500. Neill was active in the enterprise and had a list of subscriptions, dated June 3, 1851, in his personal papers. A four-room stone building was erected on the site for which the title was never conveyed to the regents.[28]

The preparatory department opened on November 26 with E. W. Merrill as principal, and with three other teachers. Expenses were met from tuition. At first, there were twenty pupils. This number grew to eighty-five in the second year. Common English branches of grammar, arithmetic, reading and spelling cost four dollars for a quarter of eleven weeks. The Higher English branches of natural philosophy, chemistry, analysis, elocution, history, astronomy, and physiology cost five dollars, and Greek, Latin, French, book-keeping and higher mathematics cost six dollars. In 1853 the regents reported that six students were pursuing the study of languages, seventeen algebra and geometry, sixteen physiology, sixteen book-keeping, twenty-nine philosophy, and six astronomy. This school struggled along until the Panic of 1857.

The Catholics in February, 1853, under the leadership of Bishop Joseph Cretin, petitioned the Legislative

Assembly to amend the School Law so that they might secure a share of the school funds for Catholic schools.[29] They complained that their children were subject to Protestant influences in the public schools. These efforts were unavailing but only after earnest debates in the legislature and after very lively public and private discussions in the community.[30]

Neill felt so deeply on the issues involved that he gave a discourse on "The Nature and Importance of the American System of Education," in the First Presbyterian Church, on Sunday morning, September 25, 1853. In response to the request of a number of citizens published in *The Weekly Minnesotian*, the address was printed in full in that paper on October 8. In it is to be found the fullest and clearest expression of Neill's ideas and convictions on public education, and on the state and the church. He began by marshalling the experiences and precedents of the Hebrews in Old Testament days to support his views on popular education.

Neill began by quoting Moses, "These words which I command thee this day, shall be in thine heart, and thou shalt teach them diligently unto thy children, and thou shalt talk of them when thou sittest in thine house and when thou walkest by the way and when thou liest down, and when thou risest up." He took as his text from the Hebrew Lawgiver these words: "What nation is there so great, and hath statutes and judgments so righteous as all this law which I set before you this day? Only take heed to thyself and keep thy soul diligently, lest thou forget the things which thine eyes have seen, and lest they depart from your heart all the days of thy life, but teach them thy sons, and thy son's sons." "Infinite wisdom," said Neill, "knew that a nation could not prosper that was not intelligent."

Neill bewailed the fact that some ecclesiastics, presumably inspired from abroad, were attacking the American public school system, and advocating the public support of sectarian schools. He declared that the states educated their children "morally and intellectually, not religiously" and that though the Constitution did not allow the Government to be a "public teacher of religion, it recognizes the system of morals that was promulgated by Jesus Christ and His Apostles." In accordance with this, he said, the states have insisted not only that a teacher be competent to teach but also that he possess a "character for morality that would make him a proper guide to youth."

"The state," however, he said, "has no more right to employ a teacher to instruct the children in relation to the Trinity of the Godhead, the disposition of all to sin, the Divinity of Christ, and the influence of the Holy Spirit, than it has to levy a tax and employ a minister of the Gospel to preach those cardinal doctrines of the Christian religion to the community at large."

The instruction in the public schools was not irreligious, just because religion was not taught. In fact, said Neill, the "explanation of the laws of nature to which he [pupil] listens, all tend to lift him from nature up to nature's God." He contended that the attribution of "godless" to the public schools was an unwarranted slur showing either ignorance or malignity.

Neill pointed out that after colonial days, the State and Church had dissolved partnership with each other, the motto of the former being "My Kingdom is of this world," and of the latter "My Kingdom is not of this world." He went on to say that the "state has no more right to inquire concerning the religious life of a teacher of a District School, than it has of the Governor of a State. If an instructor passes the requisite examination, and has a good moral character, the Trustees of the school have no right to know whether he is a Catholic, a Protestant, or an Infidel. The complexion of his faith cannot be made a test any more than the color of his eyes."

The district school, said Neill, was an institution of "*Vast Importance* to the Republic," even though it was not the place to "train up the child in the nurture and admonition of the Lord." In the first place, the school helped greatly to repress vice and crime by reducing idleness and ignorance. Secondly, he said, public instruction increased the wealth of the community by lessening the causes of pauperism and crime, and thus greatly reducing the amount of the public support of almshouses and prisons. Furthermore, he said, the wealth of a community is increased by public education because more and better work is done by those who become educated than by those who remain uneducated.

Neill stressed, in the third place, the importance of education in the inculcation of "national sentiment" and good citizenship. He pointed out how important this was for the melting pot of America, whose human components came from all over Europe to escape political or religious tyranny. In the valley of the upper Mississippi, he said, towns spring up within a few months, peopled by men from "every nation under Heaven," speaking "languages as diverse as were heard in Jerusalem on a festal day."

"The dark-eyed Italian, the blue-eyed Hibernian, the mercurial Frenchman and the high-spirited Hungarian, the contemplative German, and the hardy Norwegian, the brawny Highlander, and the reserved Englishman, are all found living together upon the prairies of the . . . West, who, only a few months [ago], were dwellers in European capitals, and accustomed to the sight of royalty and its many appendages."

These newcomers, he said, come here with both high hopes and strong prejudices. Without public education the "offspring of the emigrant, would grow up with all the peculiar prejudices their parents had imbibed in Europe." The "State by planting a common school in the midst of such a community as we have portrayed works wonders, and those in the twinkling of any eye. By taxing all the property of a community, it easily supports a school, when the Norwegian, German, or Irish, or French portion of the community would be wholly unable. It supplies a teacher that is competent to instruct the children of the neighborhood in the elements of good citizenship."

The child comes to know the history of the United

States, and "under these influences, is it not wonderful that a strong national sentiment should be fostered, and that all the children of the school should love that common country, which had afforded equal shelter and equal rights to their parents when they landed on our shores, friendless, homeless, without pecuniary resources."

After this glowing and prophetic assessment of the role of the public school for civic education, Neill said that, fourthly, "public instruction is essential to the preservation of our civil and religious liberties." He expressed the judgment that the United States was the only government in the world that had been able to "tolerate universal suffrage, and to maintain a religious faith, without any established form of religion." He attributed this to the enlightenment of the masses in the operations and purposes of the Government.

Neill proceeded to enumerate and analyze the dangers inherent in the general substitution of sectarian schools for public schools. He indicated how uneconomical, wasteful and divisive this would be in communities containing persons of several sects and of several nationalities. Such a "mutilated system," he said, would recognize the "child as a son of an Irishman, or German, or Norwegian, or as the daughter of a Baptist, Methodist, or Papist. The one [public school system] tends to promote the perpetuity, the latter the dissolution of the Republic."

The religious education of the children was the particular task of the parents and the churches, according to Neill. He pointed out that the schools only asked for thirty hours a week for secular instruction, leaving one hundred and thirty-eight hours when the children were not occupied with their "spelling books and multiplication tables." "Though the common school is important," he said, "it is of no great moral efficiency unless there is a Sunday School entirely distinct from the State, in operation by its side."

The responsibility of the churches and of the homes was made explicit by Neill. "In view of the American system of public instruction, how great the responsibility of every American Christian. The State though not opposed as we have seen, cannot give religious education even if it was so disposed. Without our youth are instructed in the principles of the religion of Jesus, though their education in the public schools may make them brilliant and ingenious, it will not make them virtuous here, but only more splendid Devils hereafter. The religious instruction of the young devolves upon the voluntary efforts of the Christian Church. What Christian parent can be excused if he does not make the words of the Bible familiar household words."

In this unusual Sunday morning "sermon" on education, Neill upheld valiantly and forcefully what he saw as some of the soundest traditions of the American way of life.

E. W. Merrill took the initiative on October 7 in calling for an "Educational Convention" for October 29, in St. Paul, to discuss this matter of publicly-supported sectarian schools. Co-signers of the call were H. F. Masterson, J. W. North, W. R. Marshall, H. M. Rice, and

[The description above is in Neill's handwriting. Neill organized this church in December, 1855. This house was pulled down in 1887, to make way for the mansion of James J. Hill.]

THE BALDWIN SCHOOL
[Courtesy of the Minnesota Historical Society]

Minnesota State Officers A.D. 1860

1 Governor Ramsey
2. Lt Gov. Donnelly
3. Secretary Baker
4 Treasurer Scheffer
5. Supt of Instruction Neill

6 Auditor McIlrath
7 Atty General Cole
8 Statistician Wheelock
9 Adjt General Acker
10 State Printer Van Vorhes

C. Seccombe. Prior to the Convention the *Minnesota Pioneer* editorialized on October 27:

This Convention is an important one, and demands the attention of those who take pride in the elevation and conduct of our schools. These schools of ours, are nursery beds, in which are planted the germs of a future generation, and unless we have skillful gardeners to nurse and train the delicate plants, they will never live to adorn and beautify our declining days. The gardeners should have good utensils to work with, for without them, weeds will grow up and choke the wheat.

When the Convention met T. R. Cressy was chosen president, and Daniel Rohrer secretary. The committee of five on resolutions included H. F. Masterson, Lorenzo A. Babcock, and E. D. Neill of St. Paul, and J. W. North and C. Seccombe of St. Anthony. Another committee of five was appointed to address the friends of education in Minnesota. Neill delivered a "short and appropriate address to the Convention."[32] The second resolution of the Resolutions Committee read: "That the tax levied for educational purposes, being expressly appropriated for the Common Schools, it cannot rightfully be applied to pay for instruction in any other schools."

In his *History of Minnesota*, Neill wrote of this issue of sectarian education: "The moderates of all denominations, and the friends of the American system of public instruction, were surprised at the introduction of a bill with such features as that introduced by Mr. Murray, and it led to considerable discussion."[33]

Neill was in Philadelphia late in 1851, seeking funds for the Presbyterian Churches in St. Paul. He advised with Rev. Albert Barnes and Dr. Thomas Brainerd concerning the desirability of establishing a private Christian academy for girls. He must have approached Mathias William Baldwin at that time on the project. Mr. Baldwin was the founder of the Baldwin Locomotive Works, and an active member of Mr. Barnes' church and Sunday School. He was a founder of the Franklin Institute for working men, founded a school for Negro children, gave liberally to various philanthropies, churches and chapels in Philadelphia, was a member of the state constitutional convention in 1837, and was elected to the state legislature in 1854.

Baldwin pledged $1500 to the proposed school and on January 4, 1852, wrote to Neill: "I like this enterprise of a good school for Females, and would be quite willing to give the sum you name for so worthy an object provided you don't lay it on too hard."[34] He demurred at the proposal to give the school his name, and counterproposed Neill's name. Mr. Barnes made a personal gift to the proposed school.

Neill was now launched on his lifetime habit of soliciting funds for worthy new enterprises, particularly educational. He had apparently concluded that the well-launched public schools in St. Paul in which he was so active, left something to be desired in the way of adequate educational advantages. He wrote to Baldwin on December 15, 1852:

Christian business men have been the builders and sustainers of every good educational institution. At the present time though the Roman Catholics have good seminaries in Galena, Dubuque and Saint Paul, the Protestants have not one. . . . It is my heart's desire to see the Baldwin Preparatory School in operation. . . . This communication may seem boyish, and enthusiastic, but I could not refrain from writing, in confidence, and if you do not approve I am sure you will not mention it.[35]

The Baldwin School was incorporated by Act of the Legislature on February 26, 1853, and it was opened shortly thereafter on Pearl Street. Neill was the president and the members of the interdenominational board were J. C. Whitney, J. G. Reihldoffer, Gideon Pond, Alexander Ramsey, William R. Marshall, Henry L. Moss, Henry F. Mastermann, and Alphius G. Fuller. Originally planned for girls, it was also made available to boys under twelve years of age.

There were twenty-eight boys and forty-three girls in attendance in the first year. The new two-story brick home of the school, between Market and Washington, was dedicated on December 29 at a gala banquet, with speeches by Governor W. A. Gorman and other prominent citizens. The trustees issued a circular for subscriptions, with flattering offers of scholarships to those contributing fifty and one hundred dollars.

Baldwin expressed a lively interest in the school and wrote to Neill on February 28, 1853:

I shall be well pleased, and satisfied if you can collect all the children in your neighborhood and give them a good religious education. What I mean is that they shall be made acquainted with the Bible and taught their duty to God, and their fellow creatures, at the same time, they acquire a knowledge of the sciences such as will make them useful in life. . . . We feel an interest in you as a Philadelphian, and as you are our representative you must make a good report of yourself. . . . I will stand by you at least, if no one else don't, so long as you need my aid, and deserve it.

The faculty in 1854 included Anna M. Paul, principal; Catherine W. Nichols, primary school; Madame Bloumer, French and German; Harriet A. Kellogg, piano; Edward D. Neill, English literature; R. H. Ewing, Latin. A New England visitor to St. Paul in the fall of 1856 wrote:

In St. Paul . . . though of recent origin . . . there is a female school of the highest grade, called the Baldwin School, which is hardly second to any in Massachusetts in the course of study, the character of teaching and scholarship, or the convenience of its appointments and fixtures. . . .

I cannot forbear to mention, in this connection, the name of one whom Minnesota, and especially St. Paul, is largely indebted for her moral and educational advantages, as well as her material growth and development. I refer to Rev. Edward Neill, one of the most devoted, indefatigable, earnest, yet modest advocates and promoters of sound morals, sound learning and true religion, whom it has ever been my fortune to meet.[36]

The educational builder was not content to stop with Baldwin School and immediately approached Mr. Baldwin concerning the possibility of establishing a college for men. The latter responded with five thousand dollars (to which he soon added five hundred more), and the ailing Rev. Barnes contributed one thousand dollars. The College of St. Paul was established with Neill as president, and with the board of trustees of the Baldwin

School. A stone building was built on Wilkin Street and the school opened to thirty-four students.

The first Bulletin of the College in 1854 announced three departments: Academic, Scientific or Practical, and, Collegiate or Classical. The "Practical Department" was something new and attested to Neill's adaptability to the temper of the times and to the needs of the frontier. "In a country so youthful," he said, "the demand is for practical men rather than complete scholars. This Department is proposed to meet the felt deficiency. It will be opened for six months of every year and will give instruction in civil engineering, chemistry of the arts and engineering, mechanics, geology, history and constitution of the United States, mercantile law and ethics." [37] The collegiate course was to cover four years, and was patterned after the courses at Yale, Princeton, and Amherst.

Baldwin suggested on June 14, 1855, that the local citizens ought to give greater support to the College. Neill replied on July 2, that they had subscribed toward a college building, and commented: "there are no active wealthy Christians here, and that the majority of the community are professional land speculators who care little for the future prosperity of Minnesota. . . . The children being educated [at the Baldwin School] are children of poor parents. Speculative money lenders in the West seem to have no children." [38]

By that time the College had accumulated a debt of one thousand dollars, concerning which Neill wrote to the church's Collegiate Society for the West, stating the predicament of the young college. He arranged for Rev. C. A. Williams and his wife to join the two institutions, Williams as head of the Academic Department, and his wife as principal of the Baldwin School, for a joint salary of one thousand dollars.

Neill was in Philadelphia in October, 1855, at which time he presented Baldwin and other friends with certain financial conditions that needed to be met before he would consent to return to St. Paul. These included back payments on his academic salary, that the debt of one thousand dollars be met promptly, that a sum be secured to erect a home for Williams, that Neill's traveling expenses for the College be paid, and that if the Collegiate Society failed to appropriate five hundred dollars for Williams' salary, this sum be otherwise assured. It is apparent that this latter appropriation was made, for three years later it was reduced to half that amount.

Neill was apparently experiencing financial difficulties of his own. His congregation had requested the American Home Missionary Society in 1853 to raise his salary to eight hundred dollars a year. The Society only appropriated two hundred dollars. In his reply to this announcement, Neill resigned his commission with the Society, and said:

A laborer . . . saith Holy Writ is worthy of his hire, and he who is apt to teach and magnifies his calling will not allow the rich church of America to obtain the privileges of the gospel or the pleasures of making the wilderness blossom as the rose, at a price less than it is worth. He will strive to exalt his profession so that men will not think ministers as beggars, and expect poor Home Missionaries to feel very "grateful" because they have left inviting fields and congenial friends at the East, to reside amid the rude and chaotic society of the West.[39]

He concluded by stating that his congregation had doubled its support during the year, and by tendering his resignation.

The College carried on but Neill records that "the development of the College was impeded by the financial revulsion of 1857."[40]

While these educational events were transpiring in St. Paul and St. Anthony, Hamline University was chartered on March 3, 1854, and was located in Red Wing. It was formally opened to men and women students in 1857, and began granting degrees in the following year.[41]

By legislative act, St. Paul became the first school district in the territory on March 1, 1856. Education was to be provided at no cost to all of its children between the ages of five and seventeen inclusive. St. Anthony followed in the next year, with provision for all children between four and twenty-one. In St. Paul, the Board of Education was created, with two members from each of the six wards. Neill was appointed secretary of the board and superintendent of schools *ex officio*, and served for three years. He designed the seal of the board, with a motto from the Greek poet Menander "Educate youth, for men you cannot." Washington School was erected in 1857 and dedicated on August 31, at a cost of about eight thousand dollars. The Adams and Jefferson Schools soon followed.

There were other developments than educational in

St. Paul in the early 1850's. The professional stage was brought to St. Paul in the summer of 1851 with George Holland and his company from Placide's Varieties of New Orleans, in Mazurka Hall. "A Day after the Fair," "Slasher and Crasher," and "Betsy Baer" were among the plays given. Sallie St. Clair with the St. Louis Varieties, was the theatrical toast of the town in 1855–7. Henry Van Liew established a permanent company in 1857 in the People's Theatre. A third company under D. L. Scott was opened and intense rivalry prevailed between the three until the crash of 1857 swept them away.[42] Amateur dramatics also flourished.

By 1853, five church buildings had been completed, and one other was in progress. The *Dakota Friend* was being published as the first religious newspaper in the Northwest, printed both in the English and in the Sioux languages. Neill frequently contributed articles. The cultural level of the citizens was attested to by the fact that there were three bookstores in the town. The Willoughby and Powers Stages were conducting the "grand tour" thrice weekly between St. Paul and St. Anthony, and some trips took in Lakes Harriet and Calhoun, Minnehaha Falls, Fort Snelling and Spring Cave.

The great Rock Island Railroad excursion came to St. Paul in June, 1854. The first railroad to unite the Atlantic and the Mississippi reached Rock Island on February 22, 1854. The contractors of the railroad staged a great celebration excursion of two trains of nine coaches each from Chicago on June 5, for the great number of invited and uninvited guests. Seven boats at

Rock Island transported at least twelve hundred persons to St. Anthony Falls, and fully one-third were turned away for lack of space. Among those visiting St. Paul were ex-President Fillmore, Charles A. Dana, George Bancroft and numerous outstanding college presidents, authors, artists, divines, geologists, and railroad men.[43]

The Panic of 1857 struck the booming pioneer town with particular severity. Seventy-five percent of the businesses and a like number of individuals were ruined. Henry T. Welles, a prominent citizen of St. Anthony and mayor in 1855, reminisced: "I don't know of one [merchant] in St. Paul or St. Anthony who weathered the storm."[44] Money almost disappeared and scrip was used for several years. Naturally, all public and private institutions suffered.

The unrealized university had a rocky time of it in these years. The later President Folwell writes of "the scandalous history of the university debt."[45] The Standing Committees of the Senate and of the House of Representatives on the University and University Lands, in 1860, reported: "In reviewing the course of policy pursued, the financial management especially can scarcely fail to meet with general disapproval." They even called the management "reckless," directed attention to the "large and costly" building that had been erected, and detailed the bad management. They believed a university to be premature.[46]

The Legislature in that year passed a bill prepared by Neill for the reorganization of the university. This provided for a board of regents consisting of the governor, lieutenant-governor, chancellor, and five persons to be chosen by the governor with the advice and consent of the Senate. The chancellor was to be elected by the regents for a seven year term. The newly-chosen board at its first meeting on April 5, 1860, elected Neill as chancellor. The Legislature then provided by law that the chancellor should be *ex officio* Superintendent of Public Instruction, although there was considerable opposition in the Senate to combining the two offices.

Because of this opposition, Neill resigned the Chancellorship on February 21, 1861. The Legislature on March 7 enacted the School Code which provided for a state superintendent of instruction to be elected by the Legislature. Neill was elected superintendent on that day by a vote of fifty-five to six. The regents at their next meeting persuaded him to withdraw his resignation as Chancellor of the University. He held both offices until July when he resigned the superintendency to take up his commission as army chaplain. The chancellorship was evidently not vacated legally until 1864, though it had become void for all practical purposes. While in office Neill had been active with Dr. J. D. Ford and others in establishing the Normal School at Winona.

The religious question in the public schools came up in a somewhat new fashion while Neill was Superintendent of Public Instruction. The Irish and German Catholic residents of a certain town petitioned the Superintendent of Schools of the town, to be set apart from the school districts in which they dwelt, because of what they felt was the Protestant character of these schools.

The local superintendent denied the petition and the Catholic citizens appealed to Neill, as Superintendent of Public Instruction.

Neill felt that the matter was important enough for an "Official Decision" which he issued on August 4, 1860. This was published in the St. Paul *Pioneer and Democrat* on August 7th. In this he said:

The fact alleged in your communication that almost all the residents of your town are Irish and Germans, and members of the Catholic Church, has not the slightest importance in the mind of the State Superintendent.

The State recognizes no man on account of his birthplace or religious preferences. She inculcates the morals of Christ in her public schools, simply because they are best adapted to promote the common weal, but she also sternly eschews the importing of distinctive dogmas of any branch of the church of Christ by any public school teacher.

An important end of the system of public instruction is to gather in a common school, the children of Irish, German and American settlers and teach them to sing national songs and love Washington, the Father of the Republic, and a greater than Washington, the Father of Spirits, and the Author of every good and perfect gift.

A republic can only exist by fostering general intelligence and urging citizens to lay aside all improper sectional and religious prejudices. . . .

While, however, it is out of my power to grant your petition, or relieve you from any taxation for school purposes lawfully imposed by your town, yet if the Superintendent of Schools in the adjoining town, and the Trustees and teachers of the nearest district are willing, it is perfectly proper for you to send your children to school in that town. . . .

Neill had resigned as pastor of the House of Hope Church on June 20, 1860, because of his duties as Superintendent of Public Instruction. This church had moved about considerably. In September, 1856, it began using the hall of the preparatory department of the College of St. Paul. In 1857 it used Irvine Hall. Its large plans for a substantial stone church to cost twenty-five thousand dollars were dashed by the Panic. The membership altered the plans in favor of a frame chapel, to cost $2775, into which the congregation moved in December, 1857.[47]

William H. Seward campaigned for Lincoln in Minnesota, September 16–19, 1860, accompanied by Charles Francis Adams and his son. In his *Diary and Notes,* the elder Adams mentioned a visit to the Minnesota Historical Society which "seems to be doing well under the care of the Secretary, Mr. Neill."[48] Thoreau was in Minnesota from May 26–June 24, 1861, accompanied by Horace Mann, Jr. In his notes, Thoreau quoted Neill, particularly on the early history of Minnesota, and on the Indians.[49] Neill had become a recognized authority in this field. His *A History of Minnesota* had been published in 1858 (enlarged and revised in 1873, 1878, and in 1882).

Neill was appointed Chaplain of the newly-formed First Minnesota Infantry in June, 1861. Neill has left a record of his address to the regiment at a very early hour on June 21st, before they embarked from Fort Snelling for the East:

. . . Your errand is not to overturn, but to uphold the most tolerant and forbearing government on earth. You go to war with misguided brethren, not with wrathful, but with mourning hearts. . . . To fight for a great principle is a noble work. We are all erring and fallible men; but the civilized world feel that you are engaged in a just cause, which God will defend. . . .[50]

He was with the regiment at the Battles of Bull Run, Fair Oaks and Malvern Hill. He resigned on July 7, 1862, and was appointed Chaplain to army hospitals in Philadelphia on July 26, 1862.

Neill became one of President Lincoln's secretaries in February, 1864, to assist in handling the President's mail, under the direction of John Hay and John Nicolay. Senator Alexander Ramsey wrote to him on September 17, 1864, "You may say to the President that he will certainly receive the vote of Minnesota. We are more and more confident of this every day." [51] Neill's personal impressions of the Civil War president were very favorable.[52] "Every month," said Neill, "my impression of the greatness of President Lincoln increased. He was above a life of mere routine. In his bearing there was nothing artificial or mechanical. . . . In conversation I never knew him to speak of himself as president. . . . He was independent of all cliques. Willing to be convinced, with a wonderful patience he listened to the opinions and criticisms of others. . . . When once opinion was deliberately formed, he was as firm as a rock. The president's capacity for work was wonderful."

Early on the morning after the election in November,

1864, Neill records: "As I passed the door of his office, which was ajar, I saw that he was at his table and engaged in official work. Entering the room, I took a seat by his side, extended my hand and congratulated him upon the vote, for my country's sake, and for his own sake. Turning away from the papers which had been occupying his attention he spoke kindly of his competitor."

At another time Neill saw him immediately after he had returned from a great fair in Philadelphia. "I found him stretched out, his head on the back of one chair, his legs resting on another, his collar and cravat on the table, a mulatto barber lathering his face, while his attorney general, Edward Bates, was quietly seated by his side, talking to him upon some matter of state. . . . To the question whether his visit was pleasant, he replied that it was, and the ladies, he believed, had made several thousand dollars by placing him on exhibition." Neill continued: "His memory was very retentive. . . . As a writer he was fluent and forcible. . . . He composed letters amid distractions which would have appalled other men. . . . President Lincoln's accessibility won the hearts of the people. . . . The last interview I had with him was between three and four o'clock of the last day of his life." After the assassination of Lincoln, Neill remained as one of the secretaries of President Johnson, to sign land patents. He resigned this position on April 25, 1867, to become chief clerk in the Department of Education, which had just been created.

Neill did not forget his educational enterprises in St.

Paul in these war years. He wrote to Baldwin from Washington on January 22, 1864, stating that he had exhausted his wife's modest patrimony in his efforts to uphold religion and education. He asked Baldwin for an endowment that would bring in fifteen hundred dollars a year, or a gift of a like amount for as long as Baldwin would live, and then continued by his executors.[53] Baldwin replied on February 2 that he could not accede to Neill's request at the time but that he might in the following year. The Minnesota Legislature on March 3, 1864, on Neill's request, amended the Act of 1853 incorporating Baldwin School, by changing its name to Baldwin University, in the expectation of a substantial endowment from Baldwin.

The locomotive manufacturer wrote to Neill on January 17, 1865, promising eighteen hundred dollars to pay the salary of a professor of the College of St. Paul for one year. Two days later he wrote to Neill that he could not guarantee fifty thousand dollars in two years, as proposed by Neill. "The money I contribute," he wrote, "depends on the success of my business. If I don't earn any, I have none to give away."[54]

Baldwin wrote to Neill on January 20, 1865, suggesting that the latter use his influence in Washington to get full payment on a claim of the Baldwin Company, with the promise that, if successful, Neill would get one-third of the amount in question, or about twenty thousand dollars, for the College of St. Paul. Neill took up the matter actively with C. A. Dana, Assistant Secretary of War, and others, with the help of Senator Ramsey, but to no avail. The decision of the Court of Claims in November, 1866, was unfavorable. Baldwin died on September 7, 1866, without leaving anything to Neill's St. Paul schools. In the next year, Neill was paying interest on a note held by the W. W. Baldwin and Company for ten thousand dollars. While Neill was in the service of the nation the Board of Education of St. Paul honored him by giving his name to the public school at the corner of Laurel Avenue and Farrington.

Neill's scholarship was productive in these years. His *Terra Mariae* or *Threads of Maryland Colonial History* was published in 1867. In the following year two volumes appeared: *Virginia Company of London*, and *Fairfaxes of England and America.*

In September, 1868, Neill was appointed by the Department of Interior, Office of Indian Affairs, to the Board of Visitors to the Red Lake and Pembina Indians, and by the Pension Office of the same Department as special agent to investigate cases of alleged fraud in Minnesota.

Neill proposed to Alexander Ramsey and W. R. Marshall in 1869 that funds of Baldwin University, which had been sold, be applied to establish a professorship in history and moral philosophy at the University of Minnesota, to which Neill would be appointed.[55] After some correspondence, Marshall wrote Neill of the Regents' meeting: "I regretted that nothing could be done to secure to the University your services."[56]

President Grant appointed Neill Consul in Dublin in September, 1869. Neill did not enjoy this work but he devoted a great amount of time to historical research and writing. His *English Colonization of America* came out in 1871. The indefatigable educator was corresponding with H. M. Knox in 1871, to propose a theological school in St. Paul. He resigned his consulship in December, 1871.

Neill returned to St. Paul after an absence of a decade, to resume his important share in the history of education in Minnesota.

Founder of a Christian College

Founder of a Christian College

EDWARD NEILL returned to Minnesota, he said, "with the determination of building up a College for young men upon a broad Christian basis." [1]

Higher education in the State had not stood still in the decade of his absence. The Methodists had chartered Hamline University in 1854 at Red Wing. The Roman Catholics established St. Johns, a Benedictine School, in 1857 at Collegeville. The Swedish Lutherans founded Gustavus Adolphus in 1862 at St. Peter. The Congregationalists inaugurated their preparatory school of Carleton College in 1867 and started college work in 1870. The Norwegian Lutherans were to establish St. Olaf's College in 1875 at Northfield. [2]

The University of Minnesota became a reality in 1869, with the coming of William Watts Folwell as president. Folwell had graduated from, and had taught mathematics, Latin and Greek at Hobart College in the state of New York, had served in the Civil War, had clerked in the store of his father-in-law in Venice, a town in northern Ohio, and had become professor of mathematics and civil engineering in 1868 at Kenyon College in Ohio. This visioned and energetic educational statesman soon got a model high school law through the Legislature providing for state aid to schools that qualified by the quality of their work. This contributed greatly to the growth of the University. The University was completely housed in "Old Main," a fine three-story structure of native blue limestone. In the early years the faculty consisted of eight professors and four assistants. The senior professor was Rev. Jabez Brooks, head of the department of Greek, formerly president of Hamline University, and graduate of Wesleyan University in Connecticut. Short daily chapel before the first class was compulsory for the small coeducational student body.[3]

Neill revived the Baldwin School in the Winslow House in Minneapolis. This hotel was built in St. Anthony in 1857, at a cost reported to be $109,000, to cater to the heavy summer trade of Southerners. Built of limestone on a high bluff it "was a 'magnificent' hotel, containing the 'most capacious and beautiful' ballroom in the West outside of Chicago. Its dining room, eighty-six by thirty-eight feet, seated five hundred people at thirty-two tables. . . . The furnishings alone were reported to have cost $45,000."[4]

Neill changed the name of the school to Jesus College and announced it as a Christian but "unsectarian" institution, "Composed of two schools: 1. The School of Christian Literature, Supplemental to the State University which is avowedly secular. 2. The Baldwin Grammar school designed to prepare students for the University of Minnesota."[5] Neill signed himself "Provost." He meant the new school to be supplemental to the University, teaching university students subjects that could not be taught in the State school.

The purpose of the college was expressed in a letter

to Mayor E. M. Wilson of Minneapolis, on November 1, 1872:

> It is hoped that in time, Christian parents will send their sons to Jesus College, where they will be under the same roof as the Provost, subject to all rules necessary to a gentle home culture, while at the same time enjoying all the advantages of University instruction at no additional expense. . . . I have thought that a supplemental school would receive a "God-speed" from Christian parents, who do not wish their sons to graduate without any critical acquaintance of the Bible; or the planting and training of the Church. . . .
>
> It [The name] has been chosen to show that the College was wholly Christian in its aim and yet designed not to interpret Christianity after the school of Luther or Calvin or Laud. The Institution is not under the supervision of the Presbyterian or any other branch of the Church. . . .[6]

President Folwell had already written to Neill, asking for copies of the advertisement of Jesus College: "I can use them possibly to our mutual advantage. I wish you the highest success and believe it will come under God's blessing with faith and patience."[7]

Tuition, board and room for a year of thirty-eight weeks in Jesus College cost two hundred and eighty dollars.[8] For two years, Neill and his sister paid the annual rent of twelve hundred dollars and met all deficiencies in current expenses. There was no evidence of public support for this plan of collegiate education supplemental to the University, and Jesus College was abandoned.

Neill now turned to Charles Macalester, the owner

of Winslow House, as a possible patron for his educational interests. This millionaire philanthropist was in his seventy-sixth year. He had been born in Philadelphia on February 17, 1798. His Scotch father was a wealthy merchant and shipowner. The son was in business in Cincinnati from 1821–1827, when he returned to Philadelphia. In 1835, he became a member of the brockerage firm of Gaw, Macalester and Company. He was a Jacksonian Democrat, and was a Government director of the United States Bank for three years. In England in 1842, he met George Peabody, the American banker of London, and became his agent in Philadelphia. He acquired large real estate holdings in Philadelphia and in western cities, particularly in Chicago.

Charles Macalester was a trusted friend of several presidents. He was an elder for many years in the Second Presbyterian Church, and then in the First Presbyterian Church, of Philadelphia. For many years he was one of the trustees of the General Assembly of the Presbyterian Church. He was a founder of the Philadelphia Presbyterian Hospital, a member of the board of trustees of Jefferson Medical College, and a trustee of the Peabody Southern Education Fund.

At first, Macalester was cool to Neill's proposals, saying that he inclined to Winslow House as a hospital rather than as a school. "The Country," he wrote in June, 1873, "is Swimming with Educational institutions, most of them crippled and always in pecuniary trouble. These are my views candidly expressed. Perhaps I may be mistaken in some, perhaps all of them. If I am, I will be glad to be corrected."[9] Neill was the enthusiast to correct him. In less than two months, Macalester was willing to give Winslow House on the condition of an adequate endowment raised locally.

Charles Macalester died on December 9, but in the Codicil to his will he transferred Winslow House to Macalester College or its Trustees, "provided that within three years from his decease, the sum of $25,000 is subscribed and paid for its endowment."[10] If the endowment was not raised the property was to revert to Macalester's residuary estate. The Codicil further stated:

> And as it is my desire that when the said property is conveyed to said College or to the Trustees thereof, it shall be held and used for no other purpose than as an educational institution. I earnestly enjoin it upon the Trustees or Directors of said College that in the event of their selling the said property at any time, the proceeds of sale thereof shall be used only in and towards the erection of other buildings for such College.

Macalester's only daughter, Mrs. Sibyl Macalester Berghman, manifested interest in the college after the death of her father. It was agreed by her and Neill that the college would be Christian but not sectarian, although two-thirds of the trustees would be Presbyterian.[11]

Baldwin College became Macalester College by Act of the Legislature on March 5, 1874. The first trustees were George L. Becker, Henry J. Horn, Henry M. Knox, Henry L. Moss, Alexander Ramsey, Edmund Rice, H. Knox Taylor, W. C. Baker, Levi Butler, Richard Chutt, W. W. McNair, J. S. Pillsbury, C. E. Vanderburg, J. C. Whitney, and Eugene M. Wilson. Eight were from Minneapolis and seven from St. Paul. All but three were Presbyterians. On December 30, 1874, Neill informed the Executors of the Macalester Estate that the $25,000 had been paid or pledged. It took some time to convince the Executors of the satisfactory fulfilment of the conditions of the Codicil.

Ever interested in popular education and with an eye to public support, Neill got permission of the board of trustees to "devote the large rooms on the main floor of the west wing of the College for the purpose of a free library, and a museum of art and natural history, to be opened for women in the morning, for students in the afternoon, and for operatives in the mills and for the public in the evening."[12]

The Baldwin School remained as the preparatory department of Macalester College. In 1874, it had classes in Greek, Latin, English, geometry, algebra, natural philosophy, history, bookkeeping, rhetoric, and "daily recitations in Bible verses and spelling." Day scholars paid twenty dollars for each of the fall and winter terms of fifteen weeks, and ten dollars for the summer term of eight weeks. Resident students paid one hundred and ten dollars for tuition and living expenses for each of the longer terms, and sixty dollars for the summer term. The nature of the school is revealed by this rule pertaining to boarding students: "Students will take their meals with the president and his family and will be expected to observe the usages which prevail among decent people. The government of the school will be paternal and all will be treated as members of a Christian family. Without permission, students will not be allowed to leave the building after supper." [13]

In his address at the installation of L. Bowman as principal of the Baldwin School on September 5, 1874, Neill said:

In the United States are three distinct and important agencies for the preparation of youth for the duties of manhood – the secular, the sectarian, and the Christian school. . . . Differing from the secular school it [Christian] teaches that the performance of duty and not merely successful achievement should be the object of life; differing from the Sectarian School, it simply placed the Bible in the hands of its students, and taught that any one who loved God and his fellow man was sure of an entrance into the Kingdom of God.

A Christian School is slower in development than the other two. It has not the pecuniary aid of the State, and it cannot appeal to the proselyting zeal of sect.

The Baldwin School . . . has always aimed to be a Christian school. . . . We hope to see accomplished a work for Minnesota as Philips [sic] Academy has done for Massachusetts. [14]

The reunion of the Old and New School branches of the Presbyterian Church in Minnesota in 1870, had strengthened the Church. The Synod in October of that year had resolved to recommend the establishment of a Presbyterian college, but nothing came of this resolution. [15]

Neill, the pioneer home missionary and pastor, left the Presbyterian Church in February, 1874, to join the Calvary Reformed Episcopal Church. He explained this decision in later years: "In the hope, that in the years to come, the Reformed Episcopal Church would be a home for many who preferred a liturgy in public worship, in 1874, Mr. Neill united with the few under Bishop [George D.] Cummins, who organized a church protesting against Sacerdotalism and Sacrementarianism."[16] Neill was a liberal in theology and he inclined toward ritualism. Furthermore, he was always susceptible to what appealed to him as a worthy new cause.[17]

In August, 1877, Neill accepted the invitation of the founders of the newly-formed Christ Reformed Episcopal Church in Minneapolis to become their pastor. The chapel was at Hennepin and Eleventh Streets. He resigned this pastorate on February 23, 1882, in a letter to the wardens and vestry, in which he said:

> For thirty years I have insisted that the day would come for a college properly endowed in the suburbs of the cities of Minneapolis and St. Paul, which would give the weight of the experience of "the wise men of the East," and inculcate that Christianity is the science of sciences, and always friendly to the most searching investigation of all phenomena, because nature and revelation are the expressions of the same divine mind. . . . In severing my connections, it is agreeable to remember that your pews have been equally open to the white, black, and red person and that no rent has been demanded.[18]

Neill had come to see that his withdrawal from the Presbyterian Church was harmful to the prospects of Macalester College, and in 1890 he returned to that Church.

Baldwin School languished in these years and Macalester College remained but a name and a hope. Neill's absence from Minnesota during the war and post-war years had put him out of touch with the newer citizens and forces. He was not too popular with some of the leading Presbyterians. His schools depended largely upon Presbyterian patronage. When Neill left the Church in 1874, he alienated much of this support, actual and potential. Furthermore, Neill had a much greater talent for conceiving plans than for executing them. He was also busy in these years with scholarly research and production.

Neill took the initiative for a meeting and banquet of about two hundred alumni of various colleges at the Metropolitan Hotel in St. Paul on January 30, 1874. A constitution was adopted, establishing the Associated Alumni of Minnesota. Neill was elected president, H. M. Knox treasurer, and William W. Folwell was on the executive committee. Seiberts band played, a male chorus sang, and there were eleven toasts.[19]

The Presbyterian Synod of Minnesota in 1878 made overtures to the trustees of Macalester College with a view to adopting the College. The trustees were willing to negotiate but the Synod felt that the president of the college should be a Presbyterian. In the course of the discussions, Neill sent in his resignation as president, to take effect whenever the sum of $30,000 was raised to endow the presidency and when a Presbyterian was chosen for the office. In 1879, Neill sought the professorship in history at the University, but President

Folwell finally replied that "the professorship of History has been virtually abolished." [20]

Affairs between the Synod and Macalester College moved rapidly to a conclusion in 1880. On January 12, Neill reminded the trustees of his offer to resign under certain circumstances, to which he added one to the effect that he would fill the professorship of History and English Literature.[21] Neill made it known that he was willing to transfer the College to the Synod provided it would remain a college exclusively for men. He was unalterably opposed to coeducation. There was, however, nothing in the charter of the College to forbid coeducation.

The final decision came at the meeting of the Synod at St. Peter, on October 15, 1880. The Committee of an Educational Institution was composed of D. W. Ingersoll, chairman, Daniel Rice, C. E. Vanderburg, and R. F. Sample. Point three of its report gave Neill's conditional resignation.[22] The Committee recommended the acquistion of the College. The Synod then, by a vote of 47-15, recognized Macalester as its educational institution.

The undenominational Christian college thus became a denominational college by the adoption of the following resolution: "Resolved that accepting the generous propositions of the Board of Trustees of Macalester College, Synod will heartily cooperate with the Trustees in the effort to speedily and liberally endow Macalester College, and do hereby recommend it to the sympathy and support of the Church under our care." No changes in the charter were suggested. A standing Committee on Cooperation with the Trustees, of seven members, was appointed with plenary powers, particularly for the purpose of appointing a financial agent. The Synod further authorized the establishment of a female college at Albert Lea and chose Rev. Daniel Rice as agent to solicit funds for both colleges.

Rockwood Macquiston became principal of Baldwin School in February, 1880, at a salary of one thousand dollars and free rent in the Winslow House. Macquiston was a graduate of Columbia College and of Union Theological Seminary, and had had churches at Winona and at Waterloo, Iowa. Extensive repairs were made in the summer at the school and open house for the Presbyterian friends of the school was held on September 30, at the opening of the fall term.

In the next year, the fall term opened hopefully enough. The faculty were Neill in Greek, history, and composition; Macquiston in Latin, mathematics, and English; and Philip A. Schaap in French and German. The committee of the trustees for the Baldwin School dismissed Schaap on August 27 "because of behaving in a disrespectful manner to the President."[23] Financial difficulties became acute and on November 25, Macquiston's resignation was accepted and the school was temporarily suspended. Neill had accumulated some wealth over the years but his generous subsidies to his schools had exhausted his means. From 1885 Neill had only his professorial income to depend on.

A syndicate formed by some of the trustees of Macalester College in 1881, bought a quarter section of land in St. Paul, known as the Holyoke Farm, bounded on the north by Summit Avenue and on the east by Snelling Avenue, for one hundred and fifty dollars an acre. The syndicate offered to the trustees an option on forty acres to be used for college buildings and a campus. This offer was accepted. The Special Committee of the Board reported on January 21, 1882: "The funds for this purpose were obtained by the pledge of securities belonging to the corporation for loans from different parties amounting to $11,000; by a loan without security of $8,000 from Rev. Dr. Rice and by a loan of $5,000 from Security Bank of Minneapolis [with the land as security therefor]."[24] Winslow House which had become surrounded by mills and factories was sold for $40,000 to the Minneapolis Exposition Company, and the Baldwin School was reopened in St. Paul.

Neill paid tribute to his New England education at the well-attended first annual banquet of the New England Society at the Nicollet Hotel in December, 1881, in response to a toast. "The speaker said . . . he had been educated in a New England college, and the influence of that New England institution he believed was stamped on his whole life."[25] Neill was ever faithful to the Amherst model in his efforts to establish a men's college in Minnesota. A few years later seven Amherst alumni organized the Northwestern Alumni Association in the Twin Cities and Neill was the oldest of its members.[26]

With his vision undimmed and with his usual op-

MRS. EDWARD D. NEILL IN 1862
[Courtesy of the Minnesota Historical Society.]

Photograph of Edward Neill and his eldest son, Samuel, taken in 1856, when Neill was secretary of the Board of Education of St. Paul. This photograph served as the model for the seal of the Board of Education. [Courtesy of Mr. Beaumont Newhall. Original in the Minnesota Historical Society.]

Macalester College, East Wing, in 1886, with Professor Charles Forbes' children in the foreground.

timism, Neill wrote to W. W. McNair, secretary of the Board of Trustees, on January 16, 1882, offering his library of five hundred volumes to the future Library of Macalester College, along with prized autographed letters of William Penn and George Washington. He continued:

It becomes us to provoke each other to good, and to go forward in the grand work of building up a broad college in this vast North-West Territory which in the words of the "Ordinance of 1787" will promote religion, knowledge and morality, the essentials of good government and the happiness of mankind, and follow the curriculum of Princeton.

The cities of Minneapolis and Saint Paul, in twenty years, at the present rate of increase [St. Paul in 1880 had 41,498, and Minneapolis 46,887 inhabitants], will contain not less than 250,000 souls, and their suburbs will touch. Between them, is the need of a center which with its library, museum, gallery of art, laboratory, observatory and faculty of professors will radiate the pure light of Christian culture and scholarship through the twin cities, to the regions beyond.

We have no college, like the one projected, in the Valley of the Upper Mississippi. The friends of education have been pleased with the prosperity of an institution which claimed to be the Oberlin of the North-West [evidently meaning Hamline or Carleton, both of which were coeducational. Oberlin opened its doors to women students for collegiate work in 1837, as the first coeducational college. In 1841, three women earned the B. A. degree as the first of their sex to do so in the United States]. All good citizens wish well to the State University supported by the proceeds of the sale of public lands, necessarily controlled by political influences, and debarred by the Constitution of Minnesota from inculcating the doctrines of Christianity, but these do not satisfy all parents, or students.[27]

He concluded by urging endowed professorships. In that year, Thomas Simpson, President of the State Normal Board, appointed Neill as chairman of the Board of Visitors to the Normal School at Mankato.

Neill resigned the presidency of Macalester College in 1884, since the synodical Endowment for the presidential chair had been secured. He accepted the professorship of history, English literature, and political economy. Rev. Thomas A. McCurdy of Wooster College was chosen president and he arrived in November to assume his duties. Shortly thereafter the three-story East Wing of the Main Building was begun. It cost thirty thousand dollars. The basement contained the dining room, kitchen, laundry, and furnace. The second floor had the classrooms, a reception room and the chapel. The third and fourth floors were used as dormitory rooms. Each floor had ten double rooms. There were bathrooms on each floor and the building was heated by steam.

The formal opening of Macalester College and the dedication of the new building were held on Wednesday, September 16, 1885, with Judge Vanderburg, president of the Board of Trustees, presiding. Trains brought several hundred people to the depot at Snelling Avenue, from which point they were taken to the college in carriages. The crowd overflowed the chapel into the hall and classrooms.[28] The choir from the Westminster

Church of Minneapolis sang and various Presbyterian pastors from the Twin Cities and from Hastings participated in the program. Neill, the founder of the College, gave the dedicatory address. Lunch was served by the ladies of the Presbyterian churches in the two cities, after which toasts were given. The thirty-six students concluded the day by organizing a baseball team.

"Thoughts on the American College" was the subject of Neill's address, and in it one finds the summation of his ideas on education, as well as a brief history of Macalester College. It reveals, too, his reconciliation of religion and science.[29]

"The dedication of a wing of a college edifice and homes for professors, which have cost about $60,000 for an American college of the type of Yale and Princeton, indicates a growth in the community. . . .

"By the American college is meant the college of the general form of Princeton or the New England college. . . . Loyalty to truth has been one of the characteristics of the American college. Truth is the expression of the divine intelligence, anywhere, and under any form. While the manifestation is varied, there is unity in the diversity, and bigots in science or theology can never effect the divorce of reason and revelation. The college delights in every discovery of the microscope or telescope; it accepts any fact fairly proved. . . .

"The trustees of Macalester College, believing in the harmony of nature and revelation, have engraved on their corporate seal two figures; one, in loose, classic drapery, standing with telescope in hand, and compass at the feet, representing science investigating the laws of nature; the other, in sitting posture, clad in modest robes, holding the open Word of God, representing revelation. Both are in friendly converse, twin sisters of heaven, as the motto suggests. 'Natura et revelato coeli gemini.' The object of the American college is not to promote an aesthetic or a medieval culture. It recognizes the life of a young man from sixteen to twenty-one years of age as most critical and susceptible. Its aim is to develop harmoniously the body, the intellect and the affections. . . ."

Turning to the teaching of religion in the private colleges Neill said: "It is to be deplored that, owing to the hostility of a sect and the opposition of unbelievers, it is impossible in our State University to have a professorship for the exaltation of Christ, and on the evidences of Christianity. . . . Now, the American College is expressly established for soul advancement, and it teaches that the system of Christ alone promotes the highest soul culture. . . . He who leaves college without the proof that Christ lived on earth, died on the cross, rose from the dead, and ascended into heaven, is a half-educated man. . . .

"No college that has been described differs from those which inculcate the forms and tenets of any particular branch of the church. . . . The American College is not built upon this narrow foundation [i.e., of the colleges of the Roman Catholic Church or Church of England].[30] . . . Macalester College teaches the doctrines of the New Testament in a way that will not offend a student who may have been trained to prefer the Baptist, Lutheran, Methodist Episcopal or Protestant Episcopal branches of the Holy Catholic church. . . ."

Neill next took a look at the true teacher. "The college professor is not what the Greeks call a pedagogue. He is not a dull man with a book in his hands mechanically hearing a recitation, watching the boys like a detective. He is very different. He is a live man in the classroom, and shows that he is a professor by a scholarly instinct, and is not attracted by the emoluments of office, and to gain the applause of fellows. His enthusiasm is imparted, the grand contagion spreads, and the college wins a name . . . the professor who did not blindly follow a text-book, but glowed all over with his theme as he sat in the class room, and caused the members, as they left and walked across the campus, to say: 'Did not our hearts burn within us while he talked to us!' . . ."

Neill's final words were on the curriculum, on intellectual discipline, on coeducation, and on high standards of scholarship. "A college student, while he may be allowed to select certain studies, must, however, conform to the curriculum which has been adopted by the professors. He is supposed to have come to college to discipline his mind by study, and the rich man's son cannot expect to find there a club house, nor are watchmen and keepers provided for any incorrigible member of a family; it can never be a lounging place, nor a reform-school. The old New England colleges only educate young men; not that they do not approve of the education of young women, but because they have thought the latter should have a higher education, which will better fit them to preside in the family, and to be the mothers of the republic. . . . The trustees of Macalester College cordially agreed to the arrangement by which a college for women should be established at Albert Lea. [He went on to speak well of Mount Holyoke and Smith College.] . . . But it should be known that the plan of Amherst and Dartmouth Colleges is the plan of Macalester. Whenever an institution of learning becomes anxious for a long catalogue of students, there is danger of its catering to the popular taste, and lowering the standard of scholarship. . . ."

President McCurdy had advocated coeducation immediately upon his arrival in the previous year. In his toast at the dedication he felt it was necessary to refute Neill's statement with reference to coeducation at Macalester. Neill took up the matter at once with the trustees and with others.[31] The matter was smoothed over by the Board. Girls were admitted to the preparatory department in 1885, but Neill refused to teach any class in which they were enrolled. The matter smoldered until 1893 but it was ever one of the sources of discord between Neill and McCurdy. Neill also resented the fact that McCurdy was not a scholarly man.

Before the College was opened, Neill's professorship in history had been taken from him, much to his displeasure.[32] When the college opened the name of the founder and senior professor was placed at the bottom of the faculty roll. Neill felt this very deeply. In December, 1884, Neill had besought the Trustees to pay the arrears in his salary, which he said had been fixed at sixteen hundred dollars a year plus fifty dollars a month for house rent.[33] Thereafter such letters were fairly frequent. Neill was becoming increasingly irascible and difficult.

Macalester College opened with thirty-six students, six of whom were freshmen and the rest were preparatory pupils in the Baldwin School. The total had grown to fifty-two in the spring term. The six freshmen were Paul McCurdy, Samuel M. Kirkwood, William P. Lee, Benjamin W. Irvin, Joseph W. Cochran, and George W. Achard. Ulysses G. Evans, James Chase Hambleton, Louis Ferdinand Slagle, and Charles Albert Winter entered subsequently and graduated with the first class in 1889. Of these ten graduates, four went into the ministry, two became missionaries, two lawyers, one a physician, and one a teacher.

In the collegiate course there were three curricula:[34] Classical, Philosophical, and Literary. Bible, English, mathematics, science, and the history of the English people were taught in all curricula, Latin and Greek in the classical, Latin and German in the philosophical, and French and German in the literary. Medieval and modern history, and international and constitutional law were available in the senior year.

Applicants for the classical course had to pass examinations in algebra through quadratic equations, plane geometry, English, grammar, word analysis, sentential analysis, geography, three books of Caesar, two books of Virgil, and one book of Cicero, or their equivalents; and, in Greek, three books of the *Anabasis* and one selection from Lucian, or their equivalents. The examinations for the philosophical course were the same except for Greek, and for the literary, excepting for Greek and Latin.

College expenses included fifteen dollars tuition for each of the three terms of twelve weeks, and three dollars a week for room, board and light. It was estimated that one hundred and eighty dollars would cover the yearly expenses.

The original faculty included Thomas A. McCurdy, D.D., Biblical Instruction and Moral Science; Rev. William R. Kirkwood, D.D., Mental Science and Logic; Rev. Nathaniel S. McFetridge, D.D., Greek Language and Literature, and Higher English and Modern Languages; Charles Forbes, B.S., M.D., Natural Science; Frank B. Pearson, A.B., Mathematics; Edward D. Neill, A.B., English Literature and Political Economy; Rev. Daniel Rice, D.D., Lecturer on the Literature and Revelations of the Bible.

Professor Pearson lived in the dormitory and conducted morning and evening devotions, in which the other professors assisted in turn. Services were conducted every Sunday morning in the chapel by the ministers in the faculty. Bible Study followed this service. Prayer meeting was held every Wednesday evening. These services were required of the students in residence.

Joseph W. Cochran[35] of the first graduating class of 1889 has characterized the original faculty members:

To the student body President McCurdy was more of a disciplinarian than anything else. . . . Dr. Kirkwood was the kindly sage and mentor . . . Dr. McFetridge was the frail and ailing classical scholar . . . Debonair Charles Forbes fascinated the students with his physical science course. . . .

Professor Pearson was the most beloved member of the faculty. He took a deep personal interest in the students and became general adviser in all extra-curricular activities, helping to organize literary societies, coaching debators or participants in oratorical contests and Shakespearian presentations and he promoted the first college journal called, *The Echo.*

Dr. Edward D. Neill, founder of Macalester College, was ripe in experience of men and events connected with our country's history. . . . It gradually dawned upon his students that here was a man who had helped to make history down in Washington and in the infant states of the upper Mississippi.[36]

The faculty chose Neill to be librarian. James J. Hill, the railroad builder, offered to give five thousand dollars for a library on the condition that a fire-proof building to cost not less than twenty thousand dollars was erected.[37] This condition was not met and Henry L. Moss gave a modest three-room, fire-proof tile building that was used as a library. Hill, however, gave thirty dollars a month for the purchase of books, beginning in 1888. He later increased this amount to fifty dollars. In 1890 he pledged fifteen thousand dollars to meet the financial crisis of that year.

The trustees built four homes on Summit Avenue between Snelling and Macalester, for professors' residences, at a cost of twenty thousand dollars. The President's salary was fixed at three thousand dollars and house, and the professors' at two thousand dollars and house.

Three hundred college alumni in the Twin Cities banqueted in the Chapel of the University of Minnesota on June 12, 1885.[38] President Northrop gave the first toast and the toast to Minneapolis was responded to by Mayor Pillsbury. The newspaper report continued:

> The toast "Commerce and Learning," was responded to by the Rev. Dr. Neill. This was one of the ablest efforts of the day. "There was a time," said the doctor, "when an impassable gulf separated the man of learning and the man of commerce. . . . The solemn-faced professor looked down upon the trader as an elongated money-bag, while the latter laughed at old 'dry-as-dust,' shuffling along the street, star-gazing or wool gathering in the poetic sense. But this has all been changed. . . . Commerce and learning are now inseparable."

In 1886, Neill received the honorary Doctor of Divinity from Lafayette College.

On the death of Professor McFetridge, Neill assumed the course in ancient history in January, 1887, and in April added the history of the English People. The professorship of history was restored to him. In the next year, Neill complained that the fifteen hours allotted to history, English literature, and political science were less than the amount allotted these subjects in any reputable institution that he knew of.[39]

James Wallace, who had joined the faculty after the death of McFetridge, to teach Greek and Anglo-Saxon, explained to Neill a mistake in the Catalogue concerning Neill's offerings and commented: "I have noticed with pain that I have suffered much in your estimation because of these mistakes."[40] Neill was also disgruntled because of the assignment of classrooms.[41] William P. Kirkwood[42] recalls that Neill once "complained stormily" for half an hour in a faculty meeting about his classroom assignment.[43]

Neill was censured by the Board of Trustees on July 3, 1890, for an indiscreet article in the *Pioneer Press* on June 24, that was critical of President McCurdy.[44] Neill denied the charges of "disrespect and insubordination" and asked for a trial. In a letter to J. C. Whitney on August 7, Neill said, "I am not an appointee of the Board of Trustees. I hold the position of Professor by compact. I accepted this trust and to the best of my ability I intend to fulfill it." The matter was smoothed out by an exchange of correspondence.

The debts of Macalester College grew steadily between 1887–1891. They increased from $37,165.34 on August 31, 1887, to $116,716.43 on January 31, 1890. The Trustees notified the faculty on July 3, 1891, that their salaries would be reduced by twenty-five per cent, beginning on September 1, "in consequence of the straitened condition of our finances."[45] President McCurdy and Rev. G. A. McAfee, the financial agent, had resigned in June. James Wallace was given administrative responsibilities as dean. Rev. David E. Platter was engaged as financial agent. He labored energetically to raise $125,000 to liquidate the debt. This was achieved by June 1, 1891.

Neill began writing and editing historical essays and articles in 1889 under the title *The Macalester College Contributions*. These were financed largely by James J. Hill, although Alexander Ramsey and Neill's son, John S. M. Neill[46] of Helena, Montana, paid for two in the series.

Student activities flourished at Macalester from the start. Beginning in 1886, *The College Echo*, an eight-page paper, came out every two weeks. It was a sheet excellent in its form, literary quality, and in the range of its college exchanges. Its editorials were well-informed and mature. In the first few years it included fraternal notes from Albert Lea College. The first volume of the annual, *The Mac*, came out in June, 1887, and was dedicated to Dr. Neill. The vigorous literary societies met on Friday evenings. The first of these, the Academian (Baldwin School), was founded on December 15, 1885, the Hyperian (collegiate) on September 24, 1886, and the Parthenon (Baldwin School) on April 15, 1887. The Y.M.C.A., Prohibition Society, Athletic Association, and the College Quartette were active in 1887. An orchestra was organized a year or two later. In 1886 the baseball team was champion in the College League of Minnesota.

In 1891, the faculty included James Wallace as dean, and Greek and Anglo-Saxon; Neill; James H. Boyd, mathematics and astronomy; Edward C. Downing, Latin language and literature; Andrew W. Anderson, mental science and English; George W. Davis, Hebrew, Biblical history and literature; Samuel M. Kirkwood, natural sciences; Niclous Bolt, German.[47]

The gymnasium was in the basement of Old Main, where handball was the principal sport. In addition to baseball, a football team was organized in 1889. The college and preparatory school students were alike eligible and even the professors played on the teams. The athletic field was in front of Old Main until the faculty and students in 1892 scraped out a new field back of Old Main.

Dr. Neill was sixty-eight in 1891, and James Wallace was forty-two. A contemporary of Neill has described him vividly at about this time:

> Mr. Neill is a well-formed gentleman physically, ordinarily tall, with light complexion, side-whiskers, and has a pleasant, courtly bearing. He not only has a very active brain, but is very active in his movements. He walks like a man on springs. . . . He is a remarkably industrious man, always either writing something or doing something ahead of public sentiment. He is constantly in advance of the world . . . yet when he is fully comprehended he is a great deal more practical than the public give him credit for. He is an earnest man, an independent man, a self-reliant man, a religious man, a progressive man, an honest man, a benevolent man, a kind-hearted man, a good man; a man of letters, a man of literature, a man of research, a man of thought; a pioneer, a worker; a human telegraph, throwing out scintillations of light; a leader of civilization. He has no conception of the value of money as personally relates to himself or to his family. . . . He is extremely sensitive as to points of honor, of true manhood, of principle. . . .

As a speaker in the pulpit or on the rostrum, Mr. Neill is earnest, sincere, clear, progressive, argumentative. He appears to be a bundle of nerves. . . .

He scorns most disdainfully anything which to him appears mean. He is thoroughly independent. He lives within himself. In person he is straight, manly, with an intellectual look, and yet one would take him to be a foreign gentleman of leisure just arrived, inspecting our institutions. . . . He has written good deeds indelibly upon the future history of Minnesota.[48]

Students have a way of bringing their professors to life. Items over the years in *The College Echo* (changed to *The Macalester Echo* in October, 1892) reveal the patriarch of the faculty. "The Doctor has the peculiar faculty of inspiring his pupils with great enthusiasm for the branches in hand. He is a historian of national reputation and gives the students of Macalester a rare privilege, by turning to their welfare. His method will be that used in the leading colleges in the East."[49] Neill was the only member of the faculty who lectured.

"On the last Sabbath of last term Dr. Neill preached a sermon from the words 'Ye are the salt of the earth' which was replete with good things. Applause seemed almost ready to burst forth on several occasions. The Doctor's sermons are always full of thought, with no air-spaces; he uses Anglo-Saxon rather than sesquipedalian English; and, therefore, he is always listened to with the deepest interest."[50]

"Dr. Neill has displayed great taste in furnishing his recitation room."[51] "Dr. Neill deserves mention as the most original member of our Faculty in his method of examinations. The plan he adopted with the Seniors in Literature and Civilization this term was to allot a certain time for each member to address the class on some subject furnished at the time by himself and chosen from the work of the term."[52] "Sometimes the engineer leaves the engine room long enough to slip into the library and listen to Dr. Neill's lectures for awhile. Then he goes back to his work and has something to occupy his thoughts the rest of the day."[53]

"The Sophomores and Juniors are kept busy these days in writing essays for Dr. Neill."[54] "The Sophomores under Dr. Neill have made marked progress this term in study of history. On December 6th his room presented a scene of unusual interest, a debate was in progress and it was necessary for the sergeant-at-arms to lock the door in order to withhold the lovers of oratory from over-crowding the room."[55] "The opening speech of the term was given by Dr. Neill, his text being, 'Go Forward!' He spoke earnestly and feelingly, and right to the point, thus commanding the attention of the students from beginning to end, as is his custom."[56] "Dr. Neill is enforcing the three-minute rule in the 'war department'."[57]

William P. Kirkwood relates the experience of December 16, 1887, when the sophomores locked Dr. Neill and his junior class in the little library where Neill was giving them an examination. Neill became very angry and started to break the door open with a hatchet. Then he refused to give the sophomores their examination scheduled for that hour until the culprit had confessed.

The sophomores chose Kirkwood as their emissary but his mission failed. A peace note, carried by a freshman, won the day, but the Doctor refused to give grades to the class for that term.[58] There are other versions of this episode, which soon became a legend of the college. *The Mac* of 1888 commented, "Beware of the fury of a patient man." Kirkwood thought Mrs. Neill was friendly but reserved and quiet. All the family were sensitive and "quick on the trigger." Neill, he said, was liked by those who knew him. Parenthetically, Kirkwood records that Dr. Wallace's enthusiasm for all things Greek, for statesmanship, for politics, and for duty made a deep impression on all students.

Joseph W. Cochran of the first graduating class of 1889, writes of Neill: "He was one of the Olympians, and to him, I think, we boys were mere mollusks."[59] In a lively and discerning reminiscence, Cochran writes of Neill:

I see a gentleman of the old school walking briskly up the board walk from the Milwaukee Station. [The Neills were then living at 515 Portland Avenue.] He has probably said a clipped, if not curt "Good Morning" to Tom Patton, the station master, as he descended from the train from St. Paul. He is wearing the conventional black frock coat and white tie of the aristocratic clergy. Of medium height and stout, he carries himself with an air of importance. No sauntering. No stopping to chat with student or professor. Business ahead!

In the class room there is none of the pedagogical chumminess, the cozy fireside attitude of modern times. The high pitched voice rasps out the names of the students with

Class of '89 in chemistry laboratory, in their junior year. J. W. Cochrane, J. C. Hambleton, S. M. Kirkwood, Paul McCurdy, George M. Achard, B. W. Irvin, W. P. Lee.

The Macalester football team of 1889, coached by Professor James Boyd. [Courtesy of W. P. Kirkwood, of St. Paul, a member of the team.]

Neill in Later Life

[Courtesy of the Minnesota Historical Society.]

machine gun velocity. Books and papers come rattling out of the black bag as tho' a trigger had been pulled. Falcon-like eyes search the terrain for the likeliest victim. The hunt for ignorance is on.

I don't wish to imply that we regarded Dr. Neill as an ogre. We were not afraid of him. But we were careful not to take liberties, for anyone out of line would be impaled upon the spot. His sarcasm was top quality.

One morning we noticed a dark cloud enveloping the good Doctor's desk. We were evidently in for a storm. It was not long before the lightning struck. Three of us had been absent for several days attending as delegates an annual convention of the State Y.M.C.A. The Doctor assumed that we had been deliberately "cutting" his classes.

"Will you young gentlemen explain your absence for the past three days?" he snapped. Conscious of our rectitude we explained our mission adding that we had been duly excused. "Pious young gentlemen, eh? Forsaking your college duties!"

What the old historian and educator lacked in *savoir faire* and adolescent psychology he more than made up in erudition and bold pioneering in the cultural development of the Northwest. His contributions to its early history and his founding of Macalester College are his enduring monuments.[60]

Edward J. Moles, now living in retirement in Minneapolis, was taken by his Quaker grandfather, Phineas M. Janney, to hear Neill preach in the Reformed Episcopal Church, when he was a boy of twelve.[61] Neill and Janney were great friends and young Moles grew up somewhat under the tutelage of Neill. He attended Neill's Sunday School class where he learned some of the catechism and "liked it." Subsequently, Moles entered the preparatory department of Macalester College in 1886, and had another year as a freshman, before transferring for a year to Princeton University.

Moles studied history under Neill, who instilled in him an enduring love of history. In his teaching, according to Moles, Neill was thorough and detailed. He was a painstaking student and a finished scholar. The students all liked Neill. He was modest and full of fun, although the students could not be familiar with him. He had a natural, "true" dignity, but students could always "feel the flutter of his humor." The "Doctor" often had students in his book-laden home, where his wife in her old-fashioned lace cap, was a friendly hostess. This "sweet" woman "sang as she talked" in her high-pitched voice. Moles recalls that students were well aware of Neill's deep opposition to coeducation.

Professor Anderson ("Prof. Andy" to generations of devoted students in more than fifty years of teaching at Macalester), who joined the faculty as a very young man in 1891, remarks that Neill was apt to break out in faculty meetings in denunciation of the Board of Trustees.[62] He wore a small black skull cap which he was prone to tear off and throw on the floor in his excitement. Neill could not get used to the preparatory school boys in the college halls. All of the other professors taught in both schools but Neill refused to do so. His sermons were scholarly and drew a good deal upon church history. They were professorial rather than evangelistic. He was friendly with students and they liked him. He had a great fund of anecdotes, stories, and historical allusions. He was a delightful social companion when he was in the right mood.

Neill, who never lacked for educational ideas, had a very pretentious scheme in 1891 for a roving Professorship of American Institutions. The chair was to be incorporated and the trustees were to be the presidents of the University of Minnesota, of Macalester, Hamline (which had moved from Red Wing to St. Paul in 1880), and Carleton, and the presiding officer of Saint Thomas Seminary. The professorship would not be filled until thirty thousand dollars were raised to endow it. The lectures would be annually delivered in "at least six places between Lake Superior and the Pacific Ocean, those in Minnesota to have the preference." [63]

If the course proved popular he suggested that Carleton inaugurate a similar course on physics and astronomy, the University on geology, botany, and agriculture, and Hamline on general history. Neill had in mind particularly "law-abiding citizens of German, Scandinavian and other foreign origin . . . who love our government, and regret that circumstances have prevented a better acquaintance with its principles." There would be no charge beyond incidental expenses.

Nothing came of the larger aspects of this proposal for adult education, but Neill made it concrete in 1891–1892, by proposing to give six lectures in Minnesota towns on "The Development of the American Government." This was welcomed warmly. The St. Paul *Pioneer Press* commented: "The American College is not a cloistered institution. Its mission is more than the teaching of young men the dead languages, in a quiet class room. It strives to be abreast with those who guide the thoughts of the community in science and philosophy. . . . It is rumored that arrangements may be made by which Dr. Neill of Macalester, will bring the college closer to the people."[64]

The St. Paul *Globe* put the matter in a novel way: "The professor of history and political economy at Macalester College is hoping to see created a movable professorship in Minnesota. . . . It appears to us this may be a beginning in the right direction, and might be supplemented by the other institutions of learning until there would be a college on wheels, constantly moving and showing that professors are not like the Dryasdust of Thomas Carlyle."

The students of Macalester acclaimed the move. "One of the greatest movements now being carried on among the universities and colleges," said *The College Echo* on October 26, 1891, "is that of university extension. . . . Dr. Neill, our professor of history and political science, is a firm believer in this great movement. . . . Is it not a rare treat for the people in the towns of Minnesota to listen to the facts of history, as they fall in such an eloquent and emphatic manner from the lips of such a scholar as Dr. Neill."

Neill gave the six lectures in the fall and winter of 1891–1892 in Red Wing, Winona, and at the Y.M.C.A. in St. Paul. They were received with enthusiasm and were reported generously in the *Winona Daily Republi-*

can, the *Red Wing Daily Republican*, and in the St. Paul papers. Much of the material in the lectures derived from original research and was at variance with some of the interpretations in the popular text books. The topics were: "The Beginnings and Some of the Democratic Elements of the English Nation"; "The Colonization of English North America"; "The Contest for Supremacy in Central North America between France and Great Britain"; "The Form and Defects of American Governments during the War for Independence"; "The Framers and Framing of the Constitution"; and, "The Administration of Washington as First President." It was appropriate that Dr. Neill became one of the earlier members of the American Historical Association in 1892.

The possibility of coeducation at Macalester College constantly plagued Dr. Neill. He was opposed in principle to coeducation and he believed deeply that it was contrary to the explicit wishes of Charles Macalester and the other founders of the college, in establishing a college exclusively for young men. Neill kept the matter steadily before the Board of Trustees and faculty. In 1889 he got assurance that girls would be admitted only to the preparatory school. Neill went out of his way to encourage and support the women's college at Albert Lea.[65]

Dr. A. W. Ringland, pastor of the First Presbyterian Church of Duluth, accepted the presidency of Macalester College in October, 1892. The College was seriously in debt. The Panic of 1892–1893 was a great calamity to the College. Dr. Ringland tried to face the crisis boldly.

In his first report to the Board of Trustees on June

10, 1893, Ringland strongly advocated at least a trial of coeducation, wholly for financial reasons. The Board decided to open the College for women. The plan was "confessedly experimental and was originally adopted for a five year trial." [66] The Board was evenly divided on the issue and only the vote of President Ringland resolved it. Two trustees resigned and some friends and supporters of the college were alienated.

James Wallace wrote to Neill on June 18 to tell him of Commencement. Neill had had to leave St. Paul at the end of May, for a rest because of an ailing heart. In his letter Wallace tried to explain the reasons for the Board's decision: "By the present arrangement we are steadily losing our constituency. When a Presbyterian daughter goes to Carleton or Hamline, we not only lose her but we lose her brothers as well if she has any. I know of case after case of this kind. Still I remember that *my* opinions on educational matters count little with you." In a note to Neill's daughter, asking her to forward the letter, Wallace wrote: "I hope he will not take the temporary admission of ladies too much to heart. Personally I have not a particle of doubt about the wisdom of the course but I am painfully conscious that my opinion weighs little with the Doctor on a question of this kind especially. The real question for two or three years has not been this or that system of education but whether the College can be saved at all." [67]

In fact, the Trustees almost closed the College. Mrs. William Thaw of Pittsburgh came to the rescue and purchased ten acres of the College property for twenty-five thousand dollars and she and her family continued to give generous support to the College. In 1893–1894, the enrollment was exactly one-hundred. In 1894, James Wallace became acting President. James J. Hill paid his salary and gave additional help. Later, he contributed ten thousand dollars, and then a like amount, to clear the college debt.

Prior to the action of the Board concerning coeducation, the students in the Hyperian Society, on February 10, had debated the question, "Resolved: that it would be for the best interests of Macalester College to institute coeducation." There was one speaker on each side followed by general debate. "On the merits of the question, the Society voted in the negative." [68] By September, the students seem to have accepted the matter gracefully. In the collegiate student body of one-hundred, there were three girls in September, 1893.

Dr. Neill protested vigorously in a formal, printed letter to the Trustees, on September 5, 1893. This summarized the history of Macalester College and the wishes of the founders and donors of the institution. Neill worked carefully on the draft of a letter to Ringland and Wallace, and finally sent it to them on September 17. In it, he said: "I never expect to desert Macalester College. . . . Whenever the Trustees inform me that college classes exclusively for young men are waiting for instruction I will be in my class room at such times as may be designated. Macalester College will never prosper until the trustees and professors will obey the Charter as worded in 1873, and carry out the wishes of the friends and donors of that time." [69] Neill was negotiating in September for a position on the faculty at the University of Minnesota.[70]

President Ringland welcomed Neill back by letter on September 23, announced a good enrollment, and inquired as to when they might expect him to meet his classes. Dr. Neill replied at once, saying: "Believing that there ought to be in the great state of Minnesota at least one College for young men, I established it. . . . The Trustees may be derelict to duty but I shall never resign, and whenever they notify me that they have reconsidered their action, I shall resume instruction in my class room." [71]

Neill died suddenly three days later in the evening of the 26th of September of a heart attack.

"Acquaintance with him," the student paper eulogized, "was accompanied always by respect, esteem and love. Quiet, modest, without pretension of any kind, he was still the pride of his fellow citizens who regarded him as the incarnation of all that was excellent and noble of the early days and a fitting exemplar of these times when his well-beloved state put off the rude garments of frontier life and clothed herself in the graceful apparel of a more prosperous era. There met in him in sweet consensus all those virtues which so adorn this transitory life." [72]

The "Apostle of Education in Minnesota" had passed away in full activity at three score years and ten.

Notes

Notes

Chapter I

[1] Folwell, William Watts, *A History of Minnesota*, 4 volumes, St. Paul, 1921–1930, Vol. IV, p. 442.

[2] Neill, Edward D., *Historical Notes on the Ancestry and Descendants of Henry Neill*, M.D., St. Paul, 1886, pp. 6–7.

[3] *Ibid.*, p. 7.

[4] Thwing, Charles F., *A History of Higher Education in America*, New York, 1906, p. 109.

[5] Cubberly, Ellwood P., *The History of Education*, Cambridge, Mass., 1920, p. 703.

[6] Thwing, *op. cit.*, pp. 112–113.

[7] *Ibid.*, p. 114.

[8] Neill Papers.

[9] Fuess, Claude Moore, *Amherst: The Story of a New England College*, Boston, 1935, p. 3.

[10] Tewksbury, Donald G, *The Founding of Colleges and Universities Before the Civil War*, New York, 1932, p. 55.

[11] *Ibid.*, pp. 66–67.

[12] *Ibid.*, p. 1.

[13] *Ibid.*, p. 5.

[14] Fuess, *op. cit.*, p. 8.

[15] *Ibid.*, p. 7.

[16] *Ibid.*, p. 30.

[17] Hammond, William Gardiner, *Remembrance of Amherst*, New York, 1946, p. 9.

[18] Fuess, *op. cit.*, p. 60.

[19] *Ibid.*, pp. 72–3.

[20] *Ibid.*, pp. 99–100.

[21] *Ibid.*, p. 100, quoting a speech of June 28, 1887.

[22] These men are described by Fuess, *op. cit.*, and by Hammond, *op. cit.*

[23] Tyler, W. S., *History of Amherst College*, Springfield, Mass, 1873, pp. 276–7.

[24] Hammond, *op. cit.*, p. 26.

[25] Neill Papers.

[26] Hammond, *op. cit.*, p. 16.

[27] *Ibid.*, p. 17.

[28] Fuess, *op. cit.*, p. 89. The Amherst General Catalogue of 1892–3, listed an alumni body of 3428 persons, of whom 1164 were ordained ministers and 120 were foreign missionaries.

[29] Neill Papers.

[30] Woods, Leonard, *History of the Andover Theological Seminary*, Boston, 1885, p. 27.

[31] Rowe, Henry K., *History of Andover Theological Seminary*, Newton, Mass., 1933, pp. 1–2.

[32] *Ibid.*, p. 14.

[33] Williams, Daniel Day, *The Andover Liberals: A Study in American Theology*, New York, 1941, p. 7.

[34] Robbins, Sarah Stuart, *Old Andover Days*, Boston, 1909, p. 3.

[35] *Catalogue of the Officers and Students of the Theological Seminary*. Andover, 1855, p. 12.

[36] *Catalogue of the Officers and Students of the Theological Seminary*. Andover, 1838, p. 9.

[37] Williams, *op. cit.*, p. 17.

[38] Jordan, Philip D., *William Salter: Western Torchbearer*, Oxford, Ohio, 1939, Ch. II.

[39] Rowe, *op. cit.*, p. 2.

[40] *Ibid.*, p. 107.

[41] *A Memorial of the Semi-Centennial Celebration of the Founding of the Theological Seminary at Andover*. Andover, 1859, p. 42.

[42] Neill Papers.

[43] *Ibid.*, Minute of a Conversation with Robert J. Poulson, November 2, 1846.

[44] *Ibid.*

[45] *Ibid.*

[46] Neill, *Historical Notes*, etc., *op. cit.*, p. 23.

[47] *Ibid.*, p. 14.

[48] *Ibid.*, pp. 14–15.

[49] Goodykoontz, Colin Brummitt, *Home Missions on the American Frontier* with particular reference to the American Home Missionary Society. See Ch. VII, "The Great Valley, 1835–55." Caldwell, Iowa, 1939.

CHAPTER II

[1] New York. Printed for the American Home Missionary Society, 1849.

[2] Quoted in Folwell, *A History of Minnesota*, *op. cit.*, I (1929), p. 250.

[3] Neill, E. D., "Saint Paul and Its Environs." *Graham's Magazine*, XLVI, No. 1, January, 1855, pp. 3–6.

[4] Bremer, Fredrika, *The Homes of the New World;* Impressions of America. 3 vols. London, 1853, Vol. II, p. 313.

[5] Blegen, Theodore C., Ed., "Impressions of Minnesota in 1849," *Minnesota History Bulletin*, Vol. V, 1923–24, pp. 286–290. The writer, "C," unknown, was in Minnesota for four weeks in the summer of 1849. His Letter, dated St. Paul, July 22, 1849, was printed in the *Eaton* (Ohio) *Register*, August 30, 1849.

[6] For a good description of the trip by boat, see Bremer, *op. cit.*, II, pp. 273 ff. She came up the river in October, 1850, on the "Menomonie."

[7] H. P. Sparhawk sent a letter from Philadelphia, dated October 16, 1849, enclosing $151 taken in a collection in the First Presbyterian Church for Neill's work. Neill Papers.

[8] Ryland, William James, *Alexander Ramsey*. A Study of a Frontier Politician and the Transition of Minnesota from a Territory to a State. Philadelphia, Harris & Partridge Co., 1941. Alexander Ramsey: born January 8, 1815; died April 22, 1903. Elected to Congress from Pennsylvania in 1843. Appointed by President Taylor governor of Minnesota Territory in 1849 for four years; Mayor of St. Paul in 1855–56; elected Governor of Minnesota in 1860; elected United States Senator in 1863 for two terms; Secretary of War under President Hayes, 1871–1881.

[9] Bremer, *op. cit.*, II, p. 283.

[10] Berthel, Mary W., *Horns of Thunder: James M. Goodhue, Frontier Editor*. St. Paul, Minnesota Historical Society, 1948.

[11] Newson, T. M., *Pen Pictures of St. Paul, Minnesota, and Biographical Sketches of Old Settlers*, etc., St. Paul, Published by the author, 1886, Vol. I, p. 75.

[12] Seymour, E. S., *Sketches of Minnesota*, New York, 1850, p. 95.

[13] McNulty, Rev. A., "The Chapel of St. Paul" *Acta et Dicta*, I, July, 1907, pp. 60–72.

[14] *op. cit.*, I, p. 256.

[15] *Journal of the Council during the First Session of the Legislative Assembly of the Territory of Minnesota*. St. Paul, 1850, pp. 68–69.

[16] Graham, Hugh, "Catholic Missionary Schools among the Indians of Minnesota." *Mid-America*, XIII, 1931, pp. 199–206.

[17] Graham, Hugh, *The History of Secondary Education in Minnesota*, University of Minnesota Dissertation, 1929, p. 22.

[18] Morton, Zylpha S., "Harriet Bishop, Frontier Teacher." *Minnesota History*, XXVIII, 1947, pp. 132–141. See Bishop, Harriet E., *Floral Home; or, First Years of Minnesota*, New York, 1857; Bliss, Frank C., *St. Paul – Its Past and Present*, St. Paul, 1888, pp. 158–9.

[19] Neill, Edward D., *Concise History of the State of Minnesota*, Minneapolis, 1887, pp. 78–79.

[20] Stevens, John H., *Personal Recollections of Minnesota and Its People,* etc., Minneapolis, 1890, p. 39.

[21] Nute, Grace Lee, ed., "A Western Jaunt in 1850." *Minnesota History,* XII, June, 1931, pp. 157–168. Letters of John Chamberlain Laird who settled in Winona, back to his family in Lewisburg, Pa., October 25, 1850.

[22] Blegen, Theodore C., "Minnesota Pioneer Life as Revealed in Newspaper Advertisements." *Minnesota History,* VII, 1926, pp. 99–121.

[23] Neill, Edward D., *A Handbook for the Presbyterian Church in Minnesota,* Philadelphia, 1856, summarizes the history of the First Presbyterian and House of Hope Churches.

[24] *Message of the Governor of Minnesota,* etc., St. Paul, 1851, pp. 8–9.

[25] In a memorandum Neill had recommended to the schools the following textbooks:

S. A. Mitchell, *The School Geographies*; R. G. Parker, *The Natural Philosophies*; W. H. Wells, *The English Grammar*; E. Willard, *The Histories of the United States*; C. Davies, *The School Arithmetic*; N. Webster, *The Elementary Spelling Book*; R. G. Parker, *The Series of Readers.*

[26] *Report of the Committee on Schools, of the Council, Accompanied by the Report of the Superintendent of Common Schools,* St. Paul, 1852.

[27] *Second Annual Report of the Superintendent of Common Schools,* etc., Saint Paul, 1853.

[28] See: "Report of the Board of Regents of the University of Minnesota," *Journal of the House of Representatives,* etc., St. Paul, 1852; Same for 1853 in *Journal of the Council of Minnesota,* etc., St. Paul, 1853; Neill Papers; Ford, Guy Stanton, *The Making of the University, An Unorthodox Report.* Minneapolis, 1940, pp. 6–7; Blegen, "Minnesota Pioneer Life, etc.," *op. cit.,* p. 114; Eide, Richard B., "Minnesota Pioneer Life as Reflected in the Press," *Minnesota History,* XII, December, 1939, pp. 398–9.

[29] "Letters of Daniel J. Fisher, A Seminarian in St. Paul," *Acta et Dicta,* I, July, 1907, p. 50. Letter written from St. Paul, February 19, 1853, to Rev. Bernard J. McQuaid, now Bishop of Rochester, N. Y.

[30] *Journal of the House of Representatives,* etc., St. Paul, 1853, pp. 130–131; 168.

[31] The original manuscript notes, in sixty-two pages in long hand, are in the Neill Papers.

[32] *Minnesota Pioneer,* November 3, 1853.

[33] Neill, Rev. Edward Duffield, *The History of Minnesota from the Earliest French Explorations to the Present Time,* 4th ed., Minneapolis, 1882.

[34] Neill Papers.

[35] *Ibid.*

[36] Gates, Charles M., ed., "The Tourist Traffic in Pioneer Minnesota." *Minnesota History*, XVI, September, 1935, pp. 275–276.

Letters published in the *Congregationalist* of Boston for September 12 and 19, 1856, and written by a New Englander recently returned from a visit to St. Paul.

[37] Macalester College, *Documentary History*. See Fawcett, Lois M., "Frontier Education," *Minnesota History*, XIV, June, 1933, p. 148.

[38] Neill Papers.

[39] *Ibid.*, Letter from Rev. D. B. Coe of New York, to Neill on August 8, 1853, on behalf of the Executive Committee of the American Home Missionary Society. Neill's reply on September 2, 1853.

[40] Neill, Edward, *Brief History of Macalester College*, St. Paul, 1885, p. 13.

[41] Tewksbury, *op. cit.*, p. 51; Kiehle, David L., *Education in Minnesota*, Minneapolis, 1903, p. 12; Asher, Helen D., "A Frontier College of the Middle West: Hamline University 1854–69." *Minnesota History*, IX, December, 1928, pp. 363–378.

[42] Whiting, Frank M., "Theatrical Personalities of Old St. Paul." *Minnesota History*, XXIII, December, 1942, pp. 305–315.

[43] Peterson, William J., "The Rock Island Railroad Excursion of 1854." *Minnesota History*, XV, 1934, pp. 405–420.

[44] Welles, H. T., *Autobiography and Reminiscences*, Minneapolis, 1899, Vol. II, p. 45.

[45] Folwell, *op. cit.*, IV, p. 437.

[46] *Report of the Standing Committees of the Senate and House of Representatives on the Subject of the University and University Lands.* St. Paul, 1860, 13 pp.

[47] *History of the House of Hope Presbyterian Church, St. Paul, Minn., 1855–1876*, St. Paul, 1876.

[48] Blegen, Theodore C., ed., "Campaigning with Seward in 1860 – From the Diary of Charles Francis Adams." *Minnesota History*, VIII, 1927, pp. 150–171; p. 161.

[49] Sanborn, Franklin Benjamin – *The First and Last Journeys of Thoreau.* Boston, 1905, Vol. II, pp. 68 ff.

[50] Neill, *Concise History, op. cit.*, pp. 195–6.

[51] Neill Papers.

[52] *Ibid.*, "President Lincoln's Mail Bag," n.d. There are many unimportant letters to Lincoln in the Neill Papers; Neill, Chaplain Edward D., "Reminiscences of the Last Year of President Lincoln's Life." Read at a Meeting of the Minnesota Commandery of the Military Order of the Loyal Legion. St. Paul, 1885, 18 pp.

[53] Neill Papers.

[54] *Ibid.*

[55] *Ibid.*, W. R. Marshall to Neill, July 2, 1869; H. L. Moss to Neill, August 9, 1869.

[56] *Ibid.*, Marshall to Neill, September 4, 1869.

CHAPTER III

[1] Neill, *Historical Notes*, etc., *op. cit.*, p. 21.

[2] In 1860, of the permanent denominational colleges in the country, the Presbyterians had 49, the Methodists 34, Baptists 25, Congregationalists 21, Catholics 14, Episcopalians 11. Tewksbury, *op. cit.*, p. 69.

[3] Leonard, Dr. William E., "Early College Silhouettes." *Minnesota History*, XVI, June, 1935, pp. 178–186.

[4] Eide, *op. cit.*, p. 403.

[5] Neill Papers.

[6] Quoted in Funk, Henry Daniel, *A History of Macalester College. Its Origin, Struggle and Growth.* St. Paul, 1910, pp. 39–41.

[7] Neill Papers. St. Anthony's Falls, April 29, 1872.

[8] Folwell, *op. cit.*, IV, p. 440.

[9] Neill Papers. Philadelphia, June 4, 1873.

[10] *Ibid.*, Philadelphia, December 23, 1873, Letter from the Fidelity Insurance, Trust and Safe Deposit Company, executors.

[11] *Ibid.*, Neill to Mrs. Berghman, December 31, 1873; Mrs. Berghman to Neill, January 8, 1874.

[12] Minneapolis *Tribune*, December 30, 1873.

[13] Buggy, Horace M., "Down Memory Lane." *St. Paul Shopper*, August 7, 1946.

[14] St. Paul *Pioneer Press*, September 6, 1874.

[15] The Minnesota Synod included in 1870, 4 Presbyteries, 80 ministers, 118 Churches, 4,764 communicants, and contributions for all purposes of $57,570. In 1880 there were 5 Presbyteries, 112 ministers, 133 churches, 6,968 communicants, and $100,235 contributed for all purposes. Funk, *op. cit.*, pp. 64 ff.

[16] Neill, *Historical Notes*, etc., *op. cit.*, p. 22. See, *Correspondence Relative to the Transfer of the Rev. Edward D. Neill, from the Presbytery of Saint Paul to the Reformed Episcopal Church*, Minneapolis, 1874.

[17] Funk, *op. cit.*, p. 36.

[18] Neill Papers.

[19] Saint Paul *Pioneer*, January 31, 1874.

[20] Neill Papers. Letter of July 30, 1879.

[21] *Ibid.*

[22] Edward, Maurice Dwight, Stated Clerk, 1855–1915, – *History of the Synod of Minnesota-Presbyterian Church USA.* 1927, p. 94.

[23] Neill Papers.

[24] *Ibid.*, Trustees Meetings, August 13, 1881; January 21, 1882.

[25] *Ibid.*, Scrapbook, newspaper clipping of December 22, 1881.

[26] St. Paul and Minneapolis *Pioneer Press*, December 22, 1888.

[27] Neill Papers.

[28] St. Paul and Minneapolis *Pioneer Press*, September 17, 1885, for a full account.

[29] Neill, Rev. Edward D.,"Thoughts on the American College." An address delivered in Macalester College Chapel, Snelling Avenue, Saint Paul, Minnesota, September 16, 1885. Also *Brief History of the College*, St. Paul, 1885.

[30] The Catholic weekly *Northwestern Chronicle* of St. Paul in a long article "The Dedicatory Services at Macalester College," on September 24, 1885, took vigorous exception to Neill's allusions to the Catholics as a sect, etc.

[31] Neill Papers. Neill to the Trustees, October 1, 1885; Neill to Rev. Dr. R. B. Abbot of Albert Lea College, September 16, 1885; Neill to Dr. Herrick Johnson, September 19, 1885; Abbot to Neill, September 22, 1885; Daniel Rice, for the Trustees, to Neill, on October 28, 1885.

[32] *Ibid.*, Thomas Cochran, Jr., to Neill, April 6, 1885; McCurdy to Neill, June 16, 1885; Neill to Trustees, June 17, 1885; Action of the Board of Trustees, July 7, 1885.

[33] *Ibid.*, Neill to Trustees, December 31, 1884; Neill to J. C. Whitney, March 20, 1885; Thomas Cochran, Jr., to Neill, April 4, 1885.

[34] *Prospectus of Macalester College, 1885–1886*. Minneapolis, 1885.

[35] Joseph W. Cochran. Graduated from McCormick Theological Seminary, had pastorates at Madison, Wisconsin, and at Philadelphia, was Secretary of the Presbyterian Board of Christian Education from 1907 to 1917, was pastor in Detroit, and Chaplain in the First World War, and from 1923 to 1933 was pastor of the American Church in Paris. Is a water colorist and author of note. Now lives in retirement at Nantucket in Massachusetts.

[36] Carson, Edward J., "Macalester's First Four Years; a Picture of the College Decades Ago," *Macalester College Bulletin*, St. Paul, October, 1945, pp. 8–9.

[37] Neill Papers. Letter from Hill to Neill, July 10, 1888.

[38] St. Paul and Minneapolis *Pioneer Press*, June 12, 1885.

[39] Neill Papers. Letter from Neill to the President and Faculty, April 6, 1888.

[40] *Ibid.*, Wallace to Neill, April 28, 1888.

[41] *Ibid.*, Neill to the Trustees, June 25, 1888; Alexander Ramsey to Neill, June 26, 1888.

[42] William P. Kirkwood was a graduate in 1890; was a member of

the faculty for a brief time, was the first and long time professor of journalism at the University of Minnesota; lives in retirement in St. Paul and is an active member of the Board of Trustees of Macalester College.

[43] Interview with the writer on November 11, 1947.

[44] Neill Papers. Letter to Neill from J. C. Whitney, communicating a resolution of the Trustees, July 5, 1890.

[45] *Ibid.*, H. K. Taylor, Treasurer, to Neill, July 5, 1890.

[46] Neill had one daughter, Minnesota, and four sons, Samuel (died in 1886), Henry, Edward Duffield, and John S. Martin.

[47] Anderson, Andrew W., "Macalester of Half a Century Ago." *Macalester College Bulletin*, St. Paul, May, 1947, pp. 11–13.

[48] Newson, *op. cit.* I, pp. 122–123.

[49] *The College Echo*, September 24, 1887.

[50] *Ibid.*, January 14, 1888.

[51] *Ibid.*, September 22, 1888.

[52] *Ibid.*, December 15, 1888.

[53] *Ibid.*, March 10, 1890.

[54] *Ibid.*, November 10, 1890.

[55] *Ibid.*, December 22, 1890.

[56] *Ibid.*, April 27, 1891.

[57] *Ibid.*, October 26, 1891.

[58] Interview with the author, November 11, 1947.

[59] Letter to the author, December 12, 1946.

[60] Letter to the author, February 20, 1947.

[61] Interview with the author, October 28, 1948. Moles remembers to this day the text of the sermon: "Fear not, little flock, for it is the Father's good pleasure to give you the Kingdom." Mr. Moles was long associated with the pioneer hardware firm of Janney, Semple, Hill and Company. His grandfather came to the Territory first in 1855, and returned in 1866. Moles' father came to Minneapolis in 1866 from Illinois.

[62] Interview with the author, December 12, 1947.

[63] Neill Papers.

[64] *Ibid.*, Clipping.

[65] *Ibid.*, Neill to Miss Margaret Stewart, Principal, Albert Lea College, November 22, 1892.

[66] Edwards, *op. cit.*, p. 214.

[67] Neill Papers.

[68] *The Macalester Echo*, February 15, 1893.

[69] Neill Papers.

[70] *Ibid.*, Letter from J. S. Pillsbury to Hon. S. J. R. McMillan, September 12, 1893. ". . . President Northrop would much like to have

Dr. Neill connected with the University; in the capacity of a lecturer. . . . I have a high admiration for Dr. Neill as a lecturer. . . . I appreciate fully, myself, the service Mr. Neill has rendered our state for many years past, and should like to see him in some position which would give him a liberal salary."

[71] *Ibid.*

[72] *Ibid.*

[73] *The Macalester Echo*, November 1, 1893.

Index

Index